Where Heaven and Earth Meet

a journey through Central Asia

Christine du Fresne

Lothian BOOKS

The documentary *Shambhala; A Central Asian Journey* is available through RB Films at www.rbfilms.com.au

Thomas C. Lothian Pty Ltd
132 Albert Road, South Melbourne, Victoria 3205
www.lothian.com.au

First published 2004

National Library of Australia
Cataloguing-in-Publication data:

du Fresne, Christine.
Where heaven and earth meet: a journey through Central Asia.

ISBN 0 7344 0613 4

1. Du Fresne, Christine – Journeys – Asia, Central.
2. Asia, Central – Description and travel. I. Title.

915.804

Colour photograph of Christine du Fresne in a Mongolian *ger* courtesy of Antonio Sa, © Antonio Sa.

Managing Editor: Magnolia Flora
Editors: Frith Luton and Magnolia Flora
Designed and typeset by Ranya Langenfelds
Printed in Australia by Griffin Press

For my mother
who taught me to love books,
and Tatyana Babanova
who suggested I write one.

Where Heaven and Earth Meet

CHRISTINE DU FRESNE was born in New Zealand and has lived in Australia for 25 years. She lives in the suburb of Ashbury, in Sydney. She has a Bachelor of Arts in Visual Arts and a Postgraduate Diploma in painting, and has been working as an artist and practising yoga for about 20 years. She teaches art at TAFE near the Blue Mountains, and for the last five years she has taught yoga in Sydney. She became a film maker with her first one-hour documentary *Shambhala: A Central Asian Journey*, which was produced by her daughter. Her documentary has been screened on ABC television and overseas. She is currently planning and researching a second film.

For my mother
who taught me to love books,
and Tatyana Babanova
who suggested I write one.

Acknowledgements

A special thank you to Garry Cousins for his generous work on the index, to Chris Ghent for his ongoing encouragement and support, and to Sally Bird who set this book in motion. Thank you also to Rosie Scott for sharing her wisdom and guiding me towards trust in my own vision; and to Pamela Horsnell, Craig Sharp, Malcolm Skewis, Simon Clark, Paul McNeill, Masoud Rowshan, Rhonda Black, Julie Taylor, Julian Noel, Antonio Sa, Elin Howe, Indigo South Czabania, Raddha Kanji, Bette Mifsud, Danny Vendramini, Ana Pedroso and Rami Shivan, who offered their help and blessings, thank you.

To the many, many wonderful Chinese, Mongolian, Tibetan, Russian, Buryat, Kazak, Kyrgyz, Uzbek, Tajik, Uyghur, Pakistani and Indian people who helped to make this journey so memorable, I offer my deepest gratitude.

And to Kylie, my wonderful daughter, thank you.

Contents

List of illustrations

The Seed

This story begins in a kitchen — a tiny, claustrophobic kitchen with no window onto the outer world of the street, in a busy cafe in Sydney where I worked as a cook. I hadn't always been a cook. It was a job I had turned to from time to time while travelling, or when thinking about my next 'career move'. But back then, at the age of fifty-one and firmly in the grip of travel fervour, following a serious career path seemed unnecessary. Cooking seemed a reasonable way to earn a living while I contemplated where my next path in life might lead me.

One day at work in the cafe one of the waitresses began to talk about the deserts of the remote interior of

Turkmenistan in Central Asia, where she had worked on an archaeological dig. She was planning to return there and brought in photographs of the deserts and ancient cities she had visited, pinning them onto the shelf above my work bench. Every day I stared at those images and was transported from the confines of the dreary little kitchen to the vast spaces and exotic landscapes that the photographs only hinted at. The images stirred deep memories of something I couldn't name but felt excited by. Inspired, we started to use Russian names for the vegetables, the appliances, the dishes and our tasks, and I began to feel that although the landscape in the photographs was both mysterious and remote, it was nonetheless accessible, and I could be there too. I remembered a small book I had picked up in a waterfront bookshop on a Greek Island five years before. It was the story of a diverse group of Europeans who travelled by horse and camel across Central Asia in the nineteenth century, during a time when the two great imperial powers of the period, Great Britain and Russia, were jockeying for control of the high mountain passes into India. The writer's words came flooding back to me:

> They were standing in the very middle of Asia. Two thousand miles to the east lay shining the city of Pekin, two thousand miles to the west rose the

> pebbled shores of the Caucasus. The world, the whole rest of the world, was far, far away. Incalculably far away.[1]

I wanted passionately to be 'far, far away' and to experience the vastness of Central Asia. The waitress's plans to travel to Central Asia fell through, but mine kept expanding.

A paragraph in a guidebook I was idly flicking through further inspired me. It contained a brief description of the Altai mountains, a range that spreads across the borders of Kazakstan, China, Russia and Mongolia. The range's highest peak is Mount Belukha, supposedly the site of a legendary earthly paradise where love and wisdom reign and injustice is unknown: *Shambhala*, the Sanskrit word for 'the place of peace, of tranquillity' — a place where heaven and earth meet. Would it be possible for me to find it?

I didn't expect to stumble across a golden city in a verdant valley surrounded by gleaming snow-covered peaks, although Buddhist Tantric art of the Himalayas often depicts Shambhala this way. I was interested in the idea that a place which has been given such enormous spiritual significance might be a very special place to visit. However, its physical location has been widely debated by scholars, and each culture in Central Asia has chosen a different mountain to mark this place of peace. The Kyrgyz have selected Muztagh Ata in the Pamir mountains of far western China, the Chinese revere a peak in the Kunluns on the eastern edge of the Tibetan Plateau, Mongolian legends speak of the Isle of Shambhaling in the great northern sea (now the Gobi Desert), Siberian shamans say that Mount Belukha is the site of Shambhala, and Mount Kailash in Tibet is revered by the Bon people as the sacred mountain. I wondered whether Shambhala encompassed the entire region of Central Asia. I planned to investigate the myth by taking a circuitous route to Mount Belukha around the heart of the largest landmass on Earth and go to as many of these mountain areas as I could.

~

A few years earlier my daughter had at last become financially independent and my partner and I had parted, so I had put my belongings into storage, bought a backpack and taken off to see the world. I travelled from St Petersburg to Istanbul, New York to Madrid. I revelled in the art and architecture of ancient Russian churches, the medieval stone sculpture of Europe and the glorious intricacies of Islamic art. I walked in the Czech mountains, flew a paraglider in the English Lakes District, followed the trails of the Knights Templar and gnostic Cathars in France. After two years of travelling I returned to New

Zealand, the country of my birth, to spend an isolated winter as the cook at a national park lodge.

My interest in far off places began when I was a child. My parents had firmly 'left-of-centre' political beliefs and at various times subscribed to both Russian and Chinese political journals. *China Reconstructs* magazines arrived at our home sporadically over several years. Sometimes they included calligraphic poster art that my father framed and hung on our bedroom walls. My mother ran a library in our livingroom in an era when the huge silver Country Library Service vans regularly visited all the rural areas. I can still smell their interiors. If I was lucky enough to be home when the library van came I was allowed to make a small selection for the children's section of the library. Crouched in the tiny aisle between two high walls of books, with narrow silver ladders to climb to the highest shelves, I was cocooned in the smell of books. The travelling librarians seemed to be very big people, too big for their tiny libraries, but strong enough to wrestle their enormous vehicles around the narrow dirt roads. They were keen travellers and in the evening after dining with us, their tales of life on the road captivated me.

My father had a series of jobs ranging from public servant, carpenter, egg farmer and market gardener to a supplier of table grapes, until finally he was able to follow his great passion, full-time winemaking. He was a lover of classical music and a great variety of people visited our music-filled house by the sea — interesting people, boring people, hangers-on and true friends, such as Wolfgang, a German economist with a big Santa-Claus laugh, who told me that if I wanted to do something badly enough but hadn't yet learned how, I must say 'Yes! I can do that' and bluff it, then learn very fast. Among my parents' friends were scholars, writers, artists and trade unionists; as an impressionable child I imbibed their ideas, outlooks, attitudes and philosophies. One of them was a well-known expressionist painter, my older sister used to draw enthusiastically and both my parents tried their hand at drawing and painting, but I never expected that I would be an artist. Books were my passion, and had been since childhood.

As an adult I worked in libraries for several years, but eventually my path took other turns. When my daughter was ten I was living in Sydney, a single parent trying to make a living as a maker of fine leather bags. The bags I made were unusual — pod-shaped to fit snugly under the armpit, the leather gathered, pleated or tucked to give a soft, voluminous look, decorated with intricately woven plaits and buttons. The one I carried drew the attention of a clairvoyant I visited once in an hour of need. 'I see you riding fast, supremely confident on your horse, across a vast plain, perhaps in Mongolia,' she said. She thought the bag had a Central Asian look, although I had never investigated the leatherwork of that area. I was sceptical. The idea of being able to ride like the wind was immensely attractive, but I'd never felt comfortable around horses.

Although I was happy making objects, I fell in love with painting and sculpture, when — unexpectedly — I had the opportunity to go to art school. My painting practice was always figurative, always about people. When I left art school and started to develop my own visual style, I realised my work was about the theatre of life; the private dramas that challenge our sense of being alive to the presence and feelings of others. In later years I discovered that this basic appreciation of our humanity was one of the 'Shambhala teachings' of the great Buddhist writer Chogyam Trungpa. Although there is a popular belief that Shambhala can still be found, Trungpa focuses on the image of the kingdom and its enlightened society to teach ways in which we can uplift ourselves and our society. As I set out on my search for the mythical kingdom, I had yet to discover these teachings. I was just excited to be going.

~

Central Asia is vast. For over 2000 years it was the focal point of ancient trade routes that crisscrossed the remote and often hostile lands between Asia and Europe, an area collectively known as the Silk Road. But it is not just a

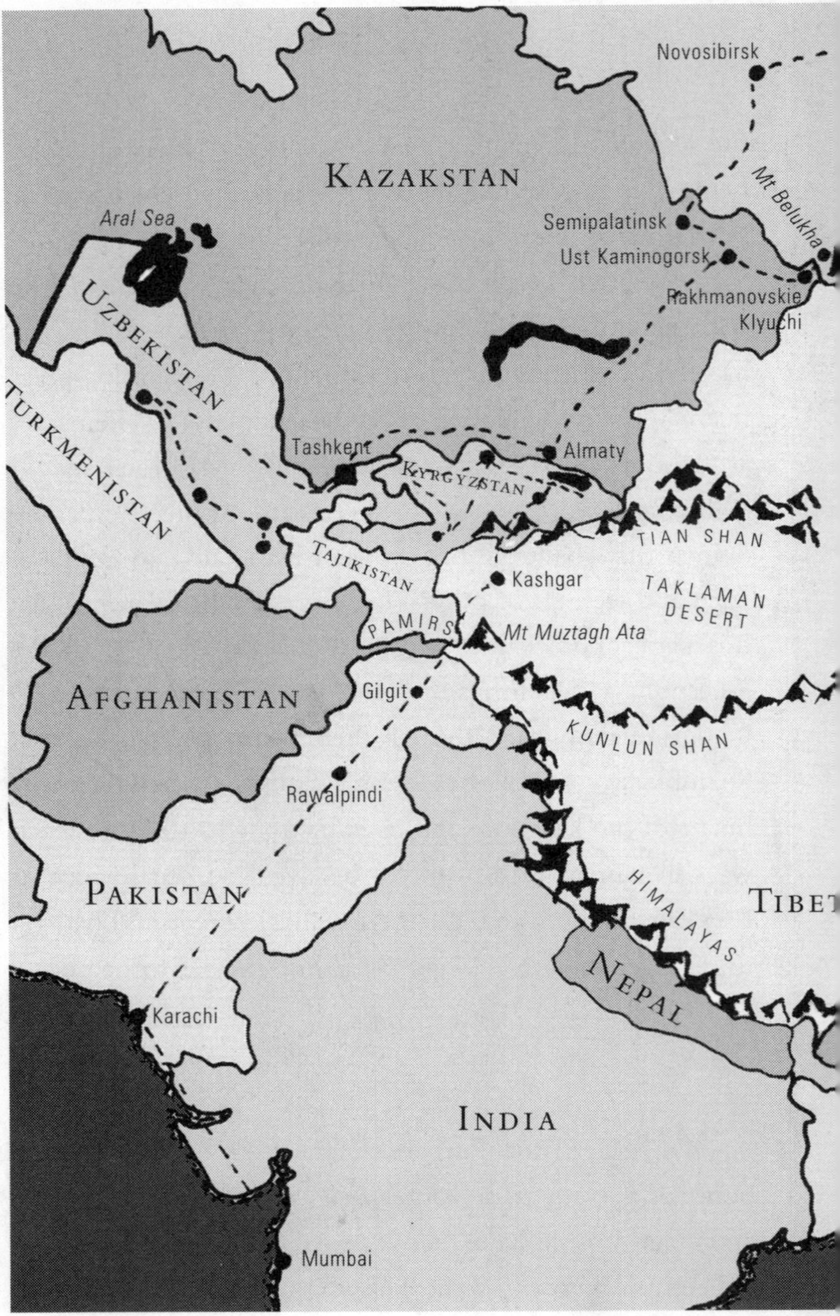
Novosibirsk
KAZAKSTAN
Mt Belukha
Aral Sea
Semipalatinsk
Ust Kaminogorsk
Rakhmanovskie
Klyuchi
UZBEKISTAN
TURKMENISTAN
Tashkent
Almaty
KYRGYZSTAN
TIAN SHAN
TAJIKISTAN
Kashgar
TAKLAMAN
DESERT
PAMIRS
Mt Muztagh Ata
Gilgit
AFGHANISTAN
KUNLUN SHAN
Rawalpindi
PAKISTAN
HIMALAYAS
NEPAL
Karachi
INDIA
Mumbai

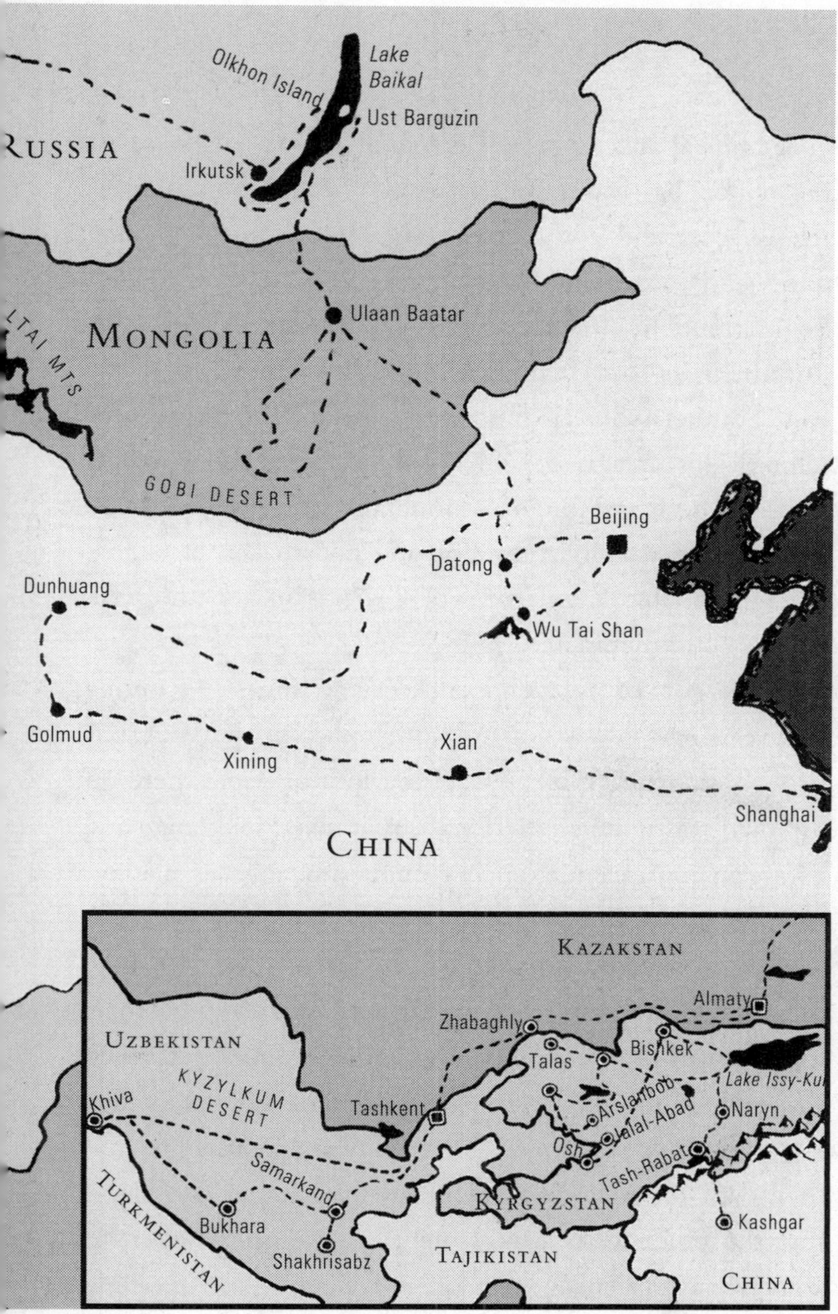

Central Asia

geographical area or an ancient highway with oasis cafes; the region has had a strong focus on scholarship, power, religion, art and commerce, and a rich history of conquest and settlement. Today, it encompasses the former Soviet republics of Kazakstan, Uzbekistan, Kyrgyzstan, Turkmenistan and Tajikistan, as well as Mongolia in the east, Southern Siberia in the north, and north-western China. This area is roughly oval in shape and contains some of the world's highest mountains, and five deserts — the Gobi of Mongolia, the Lop and Taklamakan of China, the inhospitable Kyzyl Kum of Uzbekistan and the Kara Kum of Turkmenistan.

This part of the world still sees few tourists — until a few years ago it was not only unfamiliar to the West, but also largely inaccessible — and the idea of being there on my own was quite scary. It was so far away, so strange and exotic in my imagination but unquestionably fascinating. In spite of my fears I felt irresistably drawn to go, and I wanted to have the unique experience of travelling there on my own. A lone traveller will rely on meeting others for information and companionship. Whenever I travelled alone the locals frequently wanted to look after me, offering shelter, conversation and incomparable insights into their own cultures. On this journey I wanted to find places that the guidebooks barely mention, and to be open to whatever experiences were offered. This meant travelling independently, free of any pre-booked tours and whenever possible using local transport.

I had no desire to go into the Lop or Taklamakan deserts — nor would I be allowed to. The People's Republic of China reputedly tests nuclear weapons in the Lop, and the Taklamakan has swallowed whole caravans of travellers over the centuries in its moving oceans of sand. But later I would arrive at two of the most important oases on the perimeter of this area, described as a 'very abomination of desolation' by a one-time resident of the oasis town of Kashgar. I would cross the barren Kyzyl Kum by car on my way to the ancient Uzbek city of Khiva. And in the Gobi Desert, serenely happy in a landscape of silence and stillness, a single event would change my life.

~

One evening, three months before I left Sydney, my daughter telephoned me. She is a film producer and she suggested quite casually, 'Mum, you're going on this amazing trip, why don't you take a professional video camera with you and we'll make a documentary together when you come back?'

I was familiar with a stills camera, but I had never handled a video camera, let alone shot a sequence. I knew I had a good eye for framing images, but good pictures don't necessarily make a good film. Wolfgang's advice from my young adulthood sounded clearly among the excitement my daughter's words had generated. 'Yes! I can do it!' Making a documentary seemed like a good idea.

As the time of my departure approached my friends expressed reservations. Perhaps they believed unknown dangers lurked in the high mountain areas for a Western woman aged over fifty and travelling on her own. Words like 'too old', 'dangerous' and 'foolhardy' were never uttered, but the concerns were real enough. I was aware that the huge distance I planned to cover, the difficulty of some of the border crossings and the added weight of the video camera and accessories would all make this a challenging journey. Added to this I would need to digest and be able to recall at a moment's notice an enormous amount of information relevant to film making. It was this last element that I found particularly daunting as I struggled through fast-paced lessons in camera use and storytelling in the weeks prior to my departure. I knew where I wanted to go, but how was I to tell the story?

I love to travel, but most of all I like to wander. A 'wherever the road takes you' attitude suits me best, but the more I investigated routes in and out of Central Asia, the less it seemed to be a place where wandering was encouraged, or even tolerated. In recent years China had opened up to independent travellers, although there were still out-of-bounds areas where, it was rumoured, political prisoners were kept or nuclear weapons were tested. Russia had become even more inflexible since my visit there in 1996. Obtaining a visa required pre-booking transport into and out of the country, and accommodation. This was not at all what I had in mind — one of the great joys of travelling is discovering where you will be sleeping for the night, or not, as the case may be. I begged and pleaded, and was finally granted a visa on the basis of two train tickets and two nights accommodation. The remainder of my stay was for me to discover.

A travel agent arranged my passage to the remote Altai range in northern Kazakstan, and put me in touch with a man in the south of Kazakstan who would help me with visas for Uzbekistan. There were warnings in the guidebooks for would-be travellers — 'don't fall foul of the Public Security Bureau in China by failing to renew your visa in good time'; 'if you cross this or that border expect bribery and corruption'; 'avoid this consulate and expect ridiculous delays in that consulate.' It was impossible to arrange everything before I departed, as I planned to be away for five months and visas issued before I left would be out of date before I reached the relevant border. Borders that keep some people in and others out are one of the greatest symbols of division we have constructed so far. They were also places where I needed to be very careful. I was just going to have to take my chances.

Moving West

I arrived in Shanghai, China, on an evening in May, to a setting sun stunningly red in the polluted air. A taxi took me through traffic-clogged streets and stalled overpasses to the Puijang Hotel on the waterfront, where I was given a bed in a sixth-floor dormitory. It was spartan but crisply clean and quiet, apart from the lift clanking and groaning behind the wall. The hotel was a stone's throw from Shanghai's famous Bund, the embankment along the Huangpu River. An evening stroll along the waterfront concourse quickly revealed that I had stepped into China's equivalent of Disneyworld. Weighing machines that sang; hundreds of flashlight photographs taken with a backdrop of the incredibly ugly Pudang Tower across the water; people calmly walking backwards as a form of exercise; and timid, romantic courting couples lurking in the shadows of the lower concourse, all played out in front of the oily river where convoys of filthy barges belching black smoke surged through the dark water. And in the grey light early the next morning, ballroom dancers sedately stepped and twirled to 'light classical' music that leaked tinnily from small speakers on the concourse. I felt alien and isolated, unable to make myself understood with even the simplest words of Mandarin. I had to begin filming, but I felt too self-conscious to set up the tripod and camera. This wasn't where I wanted to be.

In the dormitory the next day I met Toshi, a small, high-spirited Japanese woman who had come to Shanghai from Beijing for a job interview. She liked Shanghai although she'd left her German boyfriend behind in Beijing and she wasn't sure she wanted to move so far away from him. But right then she was happy to teach me a few things about the Chinese way of life — especially what food to eat, and where to eat it. I was overjoyed to meet someone who spoke both English and Mandarin.

We wandered the back streets behind the hotel until we found a street of pavement cafes — tiny rickety tables with rumpled plastic tablecloths and wobbly little stools, all squeezed around fires where rice and bean porridge and thin soups were cooking in big, old dented tins. I became a regular customer at the family-run place chosen by Toshi. I had no expectations about the quality of the food I would get to eat over the next five months. As a vegetarian I'd resigned myself to lots of bread and whatever else I could pick up, especially in Mongolia where few vegetables are grown, but here I was in heaven. Over the next few days, whenever a particularly wonderful dish was presented at the cafe, the son would write the name in Chinese characters for me.

Eventually I left Shanghai with my own menu for a banquet of dumplings and buns, stir-fries, soups and noodles — a list that just got longer the further I travelled west. I had no illusions about my ability to learn to pronounce Mandarin other than the obligatory 'hello', 'how are you' and 'thank you', mastered after a week of intensive practice. All other attempts were met with blank stares, so my cafe guide was tucked into my phrasebook and became just as indispensable. Vegetarian food has been an important component of Chinese food since the Song Dynasty (960CE–1279). It was developed as a culinary art in the Ming and Qing dynasties, and it even has three schools — Monastery, Court and Folk. My budget and lifestyle put me squarely into the latter category.

I visited the Shanghai Museum before I left the city. I was curious to find out if ancient Chinese art had been touched by philosophic or religious ideas from the high border areas of Central Asia and Buddhist India. Still struggling with a storyline for the film, I wanted to see if the art might lead me into a thematic exploration of the places where heaven and earth meet. In this museum I first encountered the art of the Northern Wei. The sculpted figures delighted me, reminding me of the gestures I had been using in my own artwork. Their graceful lines suggested influences from India. I was excited to discover that the art from this dynasty is found at many sites along the Silk Road, the route I planned to follow as I made my way into the western high country of China towards the Kunlun mountains. These fourth- and fifth-century sites were said to represent the peak of Buddhist cave art — I couldn't wait to leave town.

The Northern Wei had their first capital at Datong in modern Shanxi Province not far from Beijing. The Wei rulers encouraged the development of Buddhism, the most significant 'commodity' to be carried along the northern branch of the Silk Road. The Buddhism that reached China, however, did not come directly from the Indian sub-continent. Instead it is thought to have travelled to China via northern Pakistan — a cultural 'crossroads' region — and over the mountain passes of the Karakoram range that presented a less formidable barrier than the Himalayan mountains. Alexander the Great had colonised the area in about 330 BCE leaving a lasting Greek legacy (and quite a few red-headed offspring). It has been argued that this Gandharan culture was the first to represent the Buddha in a naturalist form. This fusion of Greek and Buddhist art moved over the mountain passes and down to Kashgar. Then it followed the Tian Shan mountains around the northern fringes of the Taklamakan Desert and onwards, through Dunhuang, to central China.

Three days after arriving in Shanghai I was on the train to Xian, my first stop on a long trek into western China. It's a twenty-six-hour trip just to Xian, but the prospect of seeing the Terracotta Warriors lightened my journey.

Xian is regarded as the start of the Silk Road, which is the route I would follow out to the west of China, and pick up again in Uzbekistan. Eleven dynasties had established their capitals here in the past. It was the first emperor of the Qin dynasty, Qin Shi Huang (260–210 BCE), whose extraordinary mausoleum yielded the treasures known as the Terracotta Warriors, which were discovered in 1974 by peasants digging a well. Since then thousands of terracotta warriors, horses and weapons have been uncovered in three underground vaults of earth and timber. Each figure is different and many hold real weapons that have been treated for corrosion, so that 2000 years later they are still sharp. The discovery demonstrates the consummate sculptural and metallurgical skills of a culture that existed over

2000 years ago. My eagerness to visit this place had much to do with my life as an artist, although it was unrelated to my search for Shambhala. But I could see how this earth-covered mausoleum of an emperor clearly obsessed about his place in the afterlife could be part of my exploration into the places where heaven and earth meet.

I travelled to Xian in Hard Sleeper Class — carriage No. 14, middle bunk No. 10. In this class, none of the compartments have doors, and six bunks are squeezed into each compartment. I was pleased I'd been given the middle bunk — the top one had no headroom and was far too close to the loudspeaker for my liking, and the bottom ones were used by everyone as seats during the day. There was much activity in the carriage, mostly eating and talking, which the Chinese seem to do very well and with great gusto. The loudspeakers were blaring and I had the rowdiest child in the carriage in the bunk below mine. There were two quiet well-behaved children with a lovely mother in the next cubicle. The mother immediately made eye contact with me, smiling and nodding and inviting me into their cubical to watch her tiny daughter perform incredible acrobatics between the bunks. I was the only Westerner.

I was up at 5.30 am to catch this train and had a few moments of panic in the street outside the hotel when several taxidrivers refused to take me to the station. I had no idea why. My pack felt huge and heavy, filled with objects I didn't normally travel with: a solar battery charger that folded neatly into a small case, essential for desert areas like the Gobi; a tripod; forty blank video cassettes as well as my stills film; spare video batteries and a mains battery charger; plus the usual paraphernalia for a long journey into unknown territory. I was nervous about carrying this load, not only because it weighed so much but also because I was convinced the success or failure of the next five months was held in these items, all zipped up into one sack. If I lost it, I may as well turn around and head home.

Before leaving my Shanghai hotel for Xian I had organised food, my sleeping bag and toilet gear into plastic bags, knowing I wouldn't have easy access to my pack once I was on the train. My pack was now stuffed under the lower bunk out of the way. I had remembered my earplugs at the last moment — sure enough, they were essential for getting any sleep at all. It was hot, claustrophobic and smoky when the airconditioning was shut off. The hyperactive, noisy boy in my cubicle who seemed bored and rather indulged was distracted momentarily by some pictures I drew for him.

Filming in an intimate space was the biggest challenge I faced on this first leg of the trip. It hadn't been such a problem in Shanghai after all — busy street scenes, the dormitory in my hotel, exterior hotel shots — although I constantly expected to be shouted at, waved on or somehow harassed. But now I had to do my first piece to camera and record life on the train. My ongoing confusion about the story I was to tell and fumbling clumsiness with the equipment didn't help. The light reading was difficult. I had to decide whether to use a shotgun microphone or rely on the inbuilt camera mike. What should I say? Should I use automatic or manual focus? And what was the length of the shot I was supposed to hold? On top of all this I felt conspicuous and self-conscious in my bright dayglo-orange shirt, chosen especially for continuity purposes. You would certainly never miss me if I was in frame. As it turned out it wasn't so difficult. With minimal instructions the young man from the bunk opposite mine filmed me at the little table by the window, while curious onlookers grinned hugely and stared as I stumbled through Take Two. It broke the ice and I moved easily from one-act circus to carriage community. Green tea was offered, and a woman from further down the carriage arrived for a conversation.

Zhenming was an astronomer and a physicist who had lived and worked in Sydney, and had been to the Narrabri observatory. She was the head of the Time and Frequency Standards division at the observatory, the time-service centre for all of China, and was returning to Xian from the Nanjing research laboratory. I never had to alter my watch over the vast distances I travelled in China, as Beijing time is used from the far west to the far east, and it was Zhenming's job to ensure that the time standards ran like clockwork. Was that why Chinese trains were always precisely on time? It was good to talk in English to an articulate, knowledgeable woman and the afternoon passed quickly and pleasantly. We agreed to meet in Xian where I could film an interview with her, and she would take me to see the Terracotta Warriors.

As we pulled slowly into Xian, a tout on the train convinced me to take a cheap room close to the station. It was certainly cheap, but it was a dank dungeon off a hallway that reeked disgustingly of toilet smells. I was too tired to go out looking for another room, dropped my pack onto the twin bed and smoothed back the orange plastic sheet taped over the hole in the frosted glass door. There was no hot water in the shower so I was taken out the back of the building, across a filthy alleyway and into the 'Physical Plant' building of a disused textile factory. I was left in a huge, dim shower block, feeling a little spooked. Old locker doors hung drunkenly open and the showerheads, as big as dinner plates, dripped constantly and loudly into the silence. I jumped as I caught sight of my reflection in a strange, cracked, grand old mirror. Feeling suddenly very vulnerable, I hurriedly washed off the grime of the train journey with one eye on the unlockable door. Later, I ate in one of the cafes in the 'brothel street' opposite the hotel, trying to ignore the cook picking her nose as she served up the meal. Then I wandered the city, preoccupied with thoughts about making my film.

I kept returning to the idea of places where heaven and earth meet and I made a firm decision to stop at some of the important sites of Buddhist cave art in China. Visiting the numerous caves and grottoes that are dotted along the Silk Road seemed a good way to explore this theme — the paintings and sculptures of representations of heaven, the symbols of the path to enlightenment and the Buddhas, celestial kings and *bodhisattvas* that would guide mortals towards enlightenment, all hidden in the dark recesses of the earth. It balanced nicely the science of astronomy, where the heavens are caught for us by radio telescopes like the hands of a giant earth clock measuring the sweep of stars across our skies.

Further north along this railway line were the Maijishan grottoes, caves that date back to the Northern Wei and Song dynasties. The Buddhist art from the Northern Wei people that I'd seen in the Shanghai Museum was still clearly in my mind, its warmth and earthiness gave it a unique character that appealed to me. I was to discover the Northern Wei were not Chinese at all, but Uyghur people who were now a minority in their homeland of Xinxiang. I knew nothing more than that, but felt a small knot of excitement in my belly. Four months later I would meet these people in Kashgar, the former capital of the Karakhanid Uyghur kingdom, now China's westernmost province. The nearest train station to the Maijishan grottoes was Tianshui.

I had visited Zhenming at her observatory and been taken to see the Terracotta Warriors, although it had been a rather disappointing day of wrong buses and huge crowds. Now I was ready to move west again. The train stations in China were some of my favourite places. There were throngs of moving people, huddles of stationary people, goose-stepping soldiers and piles of luggage in a wide assortment of containers being dragged hither and thither, or simply sat upon by impassive, patient, waiting people. The food vendors, paper sellers and shrill clamour was sometimes almost too much to bear. Filming it all was a joy, although I admit to turning away from my camera with a studied nonchalance as lines of soldiers marched by in front of it. This was a solitary anxious moment as I had no permission to film.

Amid the hubbub on Xian's station concourse I met Chiang, a tall, thin, self-conscious and obviously inexperienced tout who smilingly but nervously offered to take me on a tour of the sights of Xian. He seemed an interesting and knowledgeable man, and was a former middle-school history and geography teacher. I declined his services but accepted his directions to the Foreigners Ticket Office and bought my ticket to Tianshui. He was waiting for me outside, still smiling, polite and persistent. An hour later I had been persuaded to backtrack east to the Yellow River to his village, to visit his family, and we had agreed a price. He described his family as 'poor cave dwellers' and I suddenly recalled a small section in my guidebook describing these communities. With my interest piqued, any qualms I had about travelling into unknown territory with a stranger were laid aside. I could always tell Zhenming where I was going.

The next morning at 6.30 I met Chiang outside the hotel. The rain was bucketting down and the streets were covered in dirty water. A line of men had obviously spent the night huddled under the awning of the hotel. One man had an angry monkey tethered with a rope. Trying not to stare at the miserable scene I chased away disturbing thoughts of monkey brains as a possible menu item for wealthy diners. I felt like a privileged foreigner in my Gortex coat and boots.

We made the five-hour journey south in torrential rain. I was relieved Chiang didn't smoke, although it seemed the majority of Chinese men did. The bus was soon fugged up with condensation and cigarette smoke, wet clothes and murmured conversations into which the shrill voice of the radio cut like a blunt saw. Outside, bicycle riders churned through water up to the wheel hubs, shopkeepers crouched under dripping tarpaulins, and everyone remained cheerful. It was still raining as we climbed into the local town bus and drove another two hours into the hills. Chiang was by now relaxed and effusive — as a white woman I was a talking point in this rural, untouristed area. Chiang talked a lot. By the time a local taxi had taken us the last half-hour into the village, the unpaved roads were calf-deep in thick yellow mud. The main street of the village ran directly uphill between two rows of high mud walls that were overhung with mature trees, the road was a mire and seemed impassable. But our driver valiantly gunned the engine of his little van and we shuddered and slid our way to the top of the road to a tall gate set into the wall — Chiang's family home.

Nothing that Chiang had told me could have prepared me for what was behind those high earth walls. The big gate swung open to reveal a leafy courtyard, with semi-circular caves cut into the banks on two sides. Directly opposite the gate steep steps led up onto a plateau of apple orchards, and in the distance I could see green wheat fields. A shelter had been built over a corner of the courtyard; under it was a wood-fired oven, cooking pots and woks, and low stools. A small figure got up from one of the stools, staring at us. I could see the look of surprise on her lined face that quickly broke into a huge gap-toothed smile. Chiang's tiny seventy-two-year-old mother wasn't expecting us — there were no telephones here — but she quickly took charge, wanting us to go and rest immediately while she started producing what was to be an endless stream of simple, delicious food. No matter that we had already eaten in the town while waiting for the taxi, we would eat 'Mama's' food as well. She was delighted with the gift I had brought for her, a big bag of milk powder that Chiang had suggested, and I was given 'special tea' with my noodles.

I was too entranced to rest, and anyway I'd been sitting for hours. A long walk into the apple orchards and wheat fields revealed fertile Yellow River soil in a valley surrounded by barren hills. Chiang told me that until recently these hills had been home to large numbers of wolves which had been virtually hunted out, but he could remember when the wolves would come down into the wheat fields to hunt for hares. He thought that one of the village children had been killed by a wolf. The village used to be composed of two 'work units'. The wheat-threshing ground at the top of the village was still divided by a low mud wall, a reminder of the way times had changed — for now the land was divided up between families rather than into work units. Chiang's brother, who worked the orchard, was grafting on some new varieties of apple, as the old ones weren't selling well. Wherever space permitted, no matter how tiny the area, little garden plots were planted and the paths between were barely wide enough for my big boots. I felt relaxed and happy; it was a beautiful place.

While I was walking, sprightly Mama had been cooking again. Steamed sweet potatoes, sweet potato noodles made from the vegetable's starch at the bottom of the pot, bean porridge and huge steamed buns. We sat eating in the watery sunshine that filtered into the courtyard. Hens were pecking around my feet (they had their own cave carved into the bank). Chiang was translating the stream of questions from his brother and the neighbours who had dropped in to view the foreigner. 'Where is she from? What does she think of China? Is it very backward here compared with Australia? Isn't she afraid to be travelling alone?' I showed them my journal, and the map of the mountain areas I wanted to visit — it seemed Chiang's brother knew of Shambhala. I was surprised — I expected these people would know of the legend in which the Chinese philosopher Lao Tzu travels, some 2500 years ago, to a jade mountain paradise at the eastern end of the Kunlun mountains that he called 'Tebu Land', the source of the Daoist religion. In Tibet this same source is known as 'Shambhala', where the Buddha is said to have received the teachings of the Kalachakra, the great Buddhist doctrine. Although Shambhala as a place symbol is found in many esoteric traditions, including Vedanta and Sufism, I thought it interesting that Chiang's brother knew the Sanskrit word for the same concept.

By late afternoon Chiang's inexperience as a 'tour guide' was beginning to show. He told me he was sick of answering the same questions over and over again and began to affect director's status every time I picked up my video camera. His behaviour yielded unexpected benefits: I realised I had to take charge and assume the roles I had been avoiding. I was the director, the writer and the camerawoman, and I called the shots.

Mama insisted I sleep in the same bed as her that night — for my 'safety', although it was hard to imagine I faced any dangers from Chiang. Every adult member of the family had their own cave, and inside were large, hard brick benches covered with thin mattresses. I was not even allowed to go out to the 'hole in the ground' toilet, but had to squat over a round plastic basin at the door, indicated by some graphic gestures from Mama. At 3.15 am she was up again to cook breakfast, this time using another wood stove in the cave where Chiang was sleeping. Unable to get back to sleep, I lay and watched the misty dawn touch the yellow walls of the courtyard. Chiang and I finalised our payment over a breakfast of raw egg mixed into boiling water to make a soup. 'Very nourishing,'

Mama said firmly as I tried not to gag. I had to drink it all and could barely touch the porridge and delicious vegetable and tofu dish that followed.

As we made our preparations to leave Mama gave me a present — two presents. In her younger days she had been a weaver, and my gifts were woven cotton fabrics she had made, one a delicate square of fabric which I noticed the older Chinese women wearing on top of their heads, sometimes damp with water to keep the heat off. The other was a long heavy length of red and white cotton, and my heart sank a little as I contemplated having to carry it for several weeks. These were very special gifts, not to be entrusted to the rural Chinese postal system.

The rain continued. Chiang neglected to bring along any of the money I had given him for the return journey, and my tiredness erupted into irritation at his behaviour. Shoulders sagging and head drooping, he admitted he had no money to pay for the taxi from which we had just alighted, the bus we were about to board, or any food, all of which had been included in the price we initially agreed upon. Presumably the money was safely stashed somewhere in Mama's cave. Disgruntled, I gave him extra money, suddenly wanting to be on my own again. The bus back to Xian laboured through the slough of mud covering the roads, and the Yellow River looked perilously close to flood levels.

At the train station that evening, having finally and with great relief parted company with my, by now abject, tour guide, I gave up any thought of a leisurely wander around the Buddhist caves at Tianshui and caught a train west to Lanzhou, the capital of Gansu Province, that had been an important transport hub throughout Chinese history. In Gansu, I would need to comply with quirky provincial regulations that required all foreigners who travel by bus to be insured with the People's Insurance Company of China. That is, the government bus company would be insured against any lawsuit I might bring in the event of an accident, but I would collect nothing.

Gansu is a long thin province lying in an east–west direction, but I wouldn't be moving through it just yet. I was still determined to get as far as the eastern end of the Kunlun mountains at Golmud, the end of the railway line and the last town before Tibet. Perhaps someone in Golmud would know which mountain was Lao Tzu's holy jade mountain, otherwise known as 'Tebu Land' or Shambhala. From there I planned to head north to the Buddhist caves at Dunhuang. Then I would take a bus across the westernmost end of Gansu Province to eventually link up with the northern railway line. Apart from Lanzhou, none of the towns could provide the important travel insurance document and I wouldn't be allowed on a bus without one.

I'd forgotten it was Sunday, the day when it seems that the people in every town travel somewhere else by train. At Lanzhou the rain was still so heavy it was difficult to see halfway down the street. I braved the Sunday ticket queues and with some difficulty got a 'soft-seat' to Xining on a train due to leave in the early afternoon. There was no Foreigners Ticket Office here and no one spoke English. The ticket queues writhed like a trapped snake because of the pushing and shoving. Finding myself at last in front of the right window I put my elbows out like protective wings, stood on tiptoes and pointed at the relevant characters in my guidebook, gritting my teeth as the jostling kept my fingers jumping to the wrong destination.

I eventually located the office of the People's Insurance Company in town. It was a huge multi-storied building with a dark silent foyer, in the middle of which stood a single desk. At the desk was a solitary attendant whose job was to issue insurance policies. She appeared pleased to have something to do, and I was happy to have secured what turned out to be a tiny scrap of paper on which my travel relied.

At a street stall where bread was being fried under the shelter of an umbrella, I crouched under a sheet of dripping plastic and slurped breakfast curds with hot chilli sauce, garlic and coriander, and ate hot, fluffy bread.

Back at the station with two hours to wait for the

train to Xining, I caught up on my journal writing, blithely unaware of the interest I was generating. After some time I looked up to see a large, silent, attentive crowd in a semi-circle before me. I was getting used to being a one-woman circus so I decided to show off the contents of my journal. I'd glued pictures from travel magazines into the front of the book before I left Sydney. There were maps with my journey thus far marked with a thick line, and the route of my intended journey as a dotted line. I had written pages of notes and the entry tickets from various locations were also glued in. Pointing to each picture from the travel magazines I named the place, and traced my intended route with my finger, indicating that I was making this journey. This aroused enormous interest from the crowd so I stopped writing and showed the whole journal to whoever wanted to see it. This took about an hour.

Some of my 'audience' were from the Kumbun Monastery (Ta'er Si) in Xining, one of the six great monasteries of the Yellow Hat sect of Tibetan Buddhism: two monks with two young novices, one of whom was intensely curious about me and my paraphernalia, and had a radiant smile. One of the monks leaned close and whispered conspiratorially 'Dalai Lama' so I replied 'Yes, yes, yes', knowing it was forbidden to talk about him or even speak his name, and feeling very sad that I couldn't. Nor could I have brought some photographs of their religious leader with me as gifts. If such photographs were discovered, I would have been in serious trouble. The monk's very quiet and self-contained companion was such a beautiful man that I had to tear my eyes away for fear of seeming rude. I was looking forward to visiting the monastery.

The High Road

Sometimes the tickets you buy lead you into uncharted waters. In my Xining hotel room my day-pack, which doubled as a camera bag, was still standing where I had left it beside the bed five minutes before, but as I reached into it I knew instinctively that something was wrong. On the previous night I had taken off my money belt for the first time — it was full and uncomfortable to sleep on — and I thought it would be safe inside my camera pack, with my pack tucked into the edge of the bed while I slept with the door locked. But this morning the woman who brought the boiling water for tea and locked and unlocked the doors on this floor had not arrived for work, and as I was thirsty I went in search of hot water on the floor above. It was a foolish move.

Xining is an untamed town on the edge of the Tibetan Plateau where I had stopped en route to Golmud, at the western end of the railway line. I was in Qinghai Province in north-western China. Xining felt like a 'cowboy town', but it was home to a large Buddhist monastery and a small collection of Daoist temples tucked into the cliffs above the city. I'd planned to leave early in the morning to visit the Kumbun Monastery — after a cup of tea.

The thieves cleaned me out of cash and travellers' cheques, although they had left my passport and hadn't touched the video camera. They'd been fast, efficient and very tidy. In retrospect robbery is an interesting experience. The mind, at first frantic, tries to ascertain what exactly has happened. Then you feel stunned as the realisation dawns. But out of that a deep stillness and calm can also emerge momentarily. I remember that moment. As I finished desperately scrabbling through each pocket of my daypack, fear and anxiety dropped away for a few seconds, leaving me with an acute sense of alertness and clarity of mind. In my search for hot water I had knocked on the door of the room next to mine. The older man who was cleaning his teeth was friendly but shook his head. Another man was making steaming cups of tea. Irritated, I had stomped upstairs …

I didn't linger long in that moment of clarity. Bei-Hong, the floor manager, spoke some English and called the police, but I had already resigned myself to a reduced daily allowance over the next four and a half months. I knew that I could replace the travellers' cheques, though I could kiss my cash goodbye. But the police made it down to the only branch of the Bank of China in Xining just as the tellers were opening for business, and there in an orderly line were the two gentlemen who had been in the room next to mine — waiting to change my US dollars and cheques. The older man who had been cleaning his teeth was the faster of the two and was carrying most of the cash. In this impoverished province which is mostly high plateau country with sparse rainfall and long, hard winters my US$600 must have seemed like a fortune.

The other man wasn't so lucky. I saw him later that day in the police chief's office, where Bei-Hong took me to make a statement. The thief was handcuffed to a pipe in the corner of the room, and was ignored while we struggled through a mountain of paperwork. It was a confronting experience. I couldn't bring myself to look at him directly, although the situation and his plight upset me. He had gone through my bags and taken every dollar I had, but it disturbed me that I had no idea of what his fate might be. I knew that crimes against foreigners are taken very seriously in China and I tried to rationalise my actions. I had to report the theft — I had no money — but I felt uneasy nonetheless. Later, the police kept me in the room while they questioned the man. I was told he kept changing his address and forgetting his name. How could I tell them it was okay, that I could manage on what I had left? They said they'd keep working, overnight if necessary, on tracing the accomplice. I guessed that meant 'working' on that small, sad, defiant man. What had I started?

~

The robbery at the hotel, and its painful aftermath in the Xining police station, occurred on my second morning in this 'wild-west' city. Some of my travellers' cheques had been retrieved from the man I'd last seen handcuffed to the pipe in the corner of the police chief's office, but most of the cheques and my cash had disappeared with the older man who had made it through the doors of the Bank of China and into the anonymity of the streets. Replacement travellers' cheques were being couriered in from Beijing, giving me two extra days in which to contemplate how to be mindful at all times. I still felt shellshocked, the refrain 'how could I have been so stupid?' continued to play in my thoughts. But all was not grim in Xining.

I borrowed some money from Bei-Hong and took

the local bus to the Daoist temples of Beichan Si' which is still a working complex of temples, tucked into the cliffs above the city. I watched local woodcarvers at work restoring intricately carved panels, and burned incense in one of the top temples, bowing rather self-consciously three times as a gong was struck for me. I asked for a safe path, and not to lose my way (or to lose any more money). What my way was, was still unclear. I felt good leaving it in the lap of the gods for now, and while I was stuck in this town I vowed not to worry about it.

I followed a track around the mountain, panting up the steep incline as rain threatened, and suddenly I arrived at a tiny restaurant on top of the mountain. Inside, four well-dressed men played Mahjong and drank the local firewater, in a small earthen-floored room beside the kitchen. I was escorted to the kitchen to choose what I would like cooked for lunch, and invited to share food and drink with the men. Later, as their game became noisier and more spirits were consumed, I thought it prudent to head back down the hill. I was a little tipsy myself, and never worked out why these well-dressed men were sitting on top of a mountain playing Mahjong and getting smashed at lunchtime on a weekday.

From Xining, I travelled on into the western high country, across the huge deserts and saltpans of Qinghai Province to Golmud, the last big town before Tibet. I woke after a fitful sleep in a carriage that had the hardest of hard sleepers I had yet experienced. Dawn delicately lit a landscape of pure desert. Rocky outcrops were washed with soft undulations of yellow sand, and in the distance dark, rugged mountains were tinged with pink. Later, a huge saltpan — an ancient seabed — glistened with salt crystals and salt water glinted in the distance. There are many lakes in Qinghai, but only two are freshwater. Then, the first signs of the unattractive potash industry came into view. It is one of only three such sites in the world and the main reason for Golmud's existence.

Golmud is a very new city, built in the mid-1980s and, apart from the imposing sight of Mount Kunlun rising up from the plateau as though just on the edge of the city, it lacks any distinctive character. I hadn't been able to discover which of the mountains in this range had been Lao Tzu's jade mountain, and this was as far due west as I would go. If I went any further west it would have been in a minibus bound for Lhasa, the capital of Tibet. I had refused such an offer back in Xining, as I knew with deep certainty this was not how I wanted to enter Tibet — not from China, Tibet's invader.

Again I felt a little knot of excitement as I climbed onto the train. Perhaps it was in response to the good-looking foreigner I had seen crossing the platform minutes before? Over the years I had learned to trust my instincts and I felt intuitively this would be a significant trip. My carriage was almost full with a group of people who were obviously not rural Chinese, and although I hadn't specifically met any big-city Chinese intellectuals and didn't understand the language, I recognised their behaviour. I had grown up with the same sort of people albeit in a different culture. I introduced myself; some of them spoke English and I discovered they were a group of environmentalists and media people from Beijing: journalists, photographers, and a cameraman and producer from a Beijing TV station. They too were on their way to Golmud, to meet a squad of forest and wildlife police who were mostly Tibetans. The squad were fighting poachers of the Tibetan antelope, an endangered animal that lives in the high-plateau country straddling far west China and Tibet. Liang, the serious and obviously committed leader of the group, told me there were only about 50,000 to 60,000 animals left, compared with about 1,000,000 a hundred years ago. The statistics suggest that in about five or six years this animal will be extinct if the poaching is allowed to continue. The antelopes roam in a conservation area with temperatures in winter reaching –40° to –45°C and with oxygen at half the normal level. The fine underhair from the antelope's breast and throat area is smuggled via Golmud, across Nepal and into Kashmir. This is because the Kashmiri craftsmen are the best — they painstakingly weave the ultra-fine hair into scarves called *Shahtoosh*, a Persian word for 'the king of wool' — which from the late 1980s has been a highly desirable fashion item among wealthy Westerners. A kilo of this hair will fetch US$8500, which is why the hunters continue to poach — it is a fortune in this part of the world. So the special police squad, in this case the Wild Yak Patrol, have their work cut out for them, especially as this illegal trade is so difficult to detect.

The environmental group who had helped the Wild Yak Patrol with new jeeps and a radio telephone invited me to witness a public burning of about 400 antelope skins that had been confiscated from the poachers during raids on their operations. It was to take place in an area of the city believed to be sympathetic to the poachers, and was obviously calculated to teach a few people a lesson. In Golmud the next day over lunch in a local restaurant, the group (and by extension myself) were honoured guests and many toasts were made as squad members sang in honour of comrades who had allegedly been killed by the poachers. Our welcome to the city was a traditional Tibetan one. After incomprehensible but emotionally charged speeches, a white silk scarf was placed around our necks, bottles of local firewater appeared and generous shots were poured into tiny ceramic cups placed on matching trays. Many of the Beijing group were non-drinkers but it would have been discourteous to refuse the toasts, and there were amusing moments when eyeballs glazed and hands involuntarily clasped throats as fiery spirit met tender throat tissue. I was glad I was a winemaker's daughter, well trained to handle my drink. Liang's speech was long and evidently compassionate, as many of the squad members were moved to tears and I wished I had a translator, but I was told later he promised the squad their fight would become known to the Western world through my film. I resolved then and there to see this happen.

The following day, an hour before the scheduled burning of the skins, I arrived at the appointed place to find a gloomy group. It seemed the city government had suddenly decided they would not allow the pelt burning to take place within city limits. I'd been told by Liang of the difficulties inherent in Chinese bureaucracy and of the corruption that exists at many levels which often prevents clear action, particularly on environmental issues. The squad was under an obligation to the environmental group to burn the skins, so it was decided to take the skins to the squad's base high in the Kunlun mountains where the media people could complete their story, scheduled to be aired on Beijing TV on World Environment Day. I was disappointed. Was this going to be a story I couldn't finish? Was their mountain destination the Shambhala of Lao Tzu? I hadn't been invited to go into the mountains with them and, anyway, I'd already bought a bus ticket to take me to Dunhuang in the north, the following day.

That afternoon I filmed the group buying warm blankets, gloves and scarves, to be left at the squad's base after their departure. It was a five-hour drive up to the base, and at night it would be bitterly cold. I arranged to pick up video footage of the journey and the pelt burning from Beijing so I could finish my film of their story, and made my own arrangements to leave early next morning. I had a thirteen-hour bus journey to Dunhuang, and I hadn't found Shambhala.

I spent thirteen hours with my knees jammed under my chin, one of only four women on the bus. I had ample time to reflect on the larger story I had chosen to tell. The other supposed site of Shambhala I had ruled out of my itinerary was Mount Kailash in north-western Tibet, a difficult place to reach at the best of times. It now lay far, far to the west, the highest mountain in the Trans-Himalayan chain. Kailash was revered by the Bon people and was considered by many Tibetan Buddhist scholars to be the site of Shambhala, and the original source of the Kalachakra, part of the esoteric tradition of Tibetan Buddhism. But I was also becoming interested in the practical teachings that convey the wisdom of Shambhala. As Chogyam Trungpa explains in *Shambhala: The Sacred Path of the Warrior*:

> There has long been a tradition that regards the kingdom of Shambhala, not as an external place, but as the ground or root of wakefulness and sanity that exists as a potential within every human being.[2]

In this vision of Shambhala its inner significance is of a genuine, compassionate and fearless existence. The Wild Yak Patrol that I had left behind in Golmud was a perfect example. The group were mostly Tibetans living in a Chinese city on the edge of a high plateau which used to be their own country, risking their lives to save a unique animal from extinction, and waging battle on two fronts: the well-armed poachers and the well-heeled Westerners. It may not have appeared to be a very 'winnable' fight, but I knew where my allegiance lay.

~

A sea of sand dunes surrounds the oasis town of Dunhuang. A few hours before entering the town, I watched a sand storm sweep across the emptiness far to the west of the road and I remembered a story the explorer Mildred Cable tells about a Chinese priest who was travelling back to Dunhuang from a distant lake. A huge sand storm blew up at dusk and as he tried to find some shelter from the shrieking wind and driving sand, he thought he saw a light. Walking towards the light, the priest saw that it had moved further on so he followed it, passing through an opening in a cliff and down a steep path to a river. Just there the river had cut a very deep bed, and the path was treacherous in the howling wind, but he reached a ledge on the bank and found a cave where he slept.

> When he awoke it was daylight, and from the walls of the cave he saw paintings of holy men looking down on him. He tells us that he got up, explored farther and found various other small openings leading into caves hollowed from the cliff. He pushed on to Tunhwang [Dunhuang] and immediately reported the matter. Some of us went out to see the place, and found that it was as he said, and that a quantity of loose gravel, recently washed from the bank, had left these caves exposed.[3]

There are many stories of hidden caves and secret tunnels under these deserts and eroded mountain ranges, tunnels that supposedly lead to some of the major monasteries on the high plateaux of Tibet, perhaps even to Shambhala. This secret information is allegedly closely guarded by the high lamas of Tibetan Buddhism. In Dunhuang my main concern was how many of the Mogao caves would be open to the public during my brief stay. Dunhuang's position at the edge of the Taklamakan Desert — the meeting point of routes around the north and south of the desert — made it an essential stop for both inbound and outbound travellers on the Silk Road. At times it has been under both Tibetan and Uyghur rule, but modern Dunhuang is a town that lives from tourism. And what people come here to see are the extraordinary Mogao caves.

The origin of the caves goes back to 366 CE when a monk received a vision at the spot and dug the first cave. Fortunately for the history of art, Dunhuang's position as an important staging post on the Silk Road meant that there were plenty of donors to provide money for subsequent caves to be dug. Wealthy merchants, anxious to be protected from the very real dangers of the Taklamakan Desert crossing or giving thanks for a safe crossing already accomplished, would make donations as an act of merit, an act that might also enable the donor to escape rebirth into this human realm, the world of suffering.

The sandstone edges of the Taklamakan Desert hide some of the outstanding examples of cave or grotto art in the world. The Dunhuang grottoes contain both sculptural and mural art, but large quantities of ancient documents have been found there too; documents that cover a wide range of subjects, in a number of languages — Chinese, Sanskrit, Tibetan, Uyghur and others that are still unknown. And alongside the vast range of Buddhist imagery there are scenes of everyday life of the time — domestic imagery, scenes of celebration, and images depicting the difficulties of this most challenging and dangerous section of the Silk Road. Rediscovered in 1900, the caves were at first plundered by canny archaeologists, who carried off thousands of antiquities to museums around the world, but the caves are now well protected and being intensively restored.

The caves with art from the Northern Wei Dynasty were closed for restoration, and not due to re-open until later in the year. I was intensely disappointed. I was not allowed to film in any of the caves, but I found some satisfaction contemplating the Zhou Dynasty art, which in its linear abstraction was reminiscent of Romanesque art in Europe. I wanted to stay and draw but as with most tours in places of archaeological interest I was hustled along to catch up with the group. By noon all the tour groups had gone, the sun was blazing onto the reflective desert sand with a ferocity I hadn't encountered before, but the solitude was irresistible. I put on protective clothing and walked up into the dunes. A lone cuckoo was singing in the trees near the caves and bells were tinkling off the eaves of the buildings below. Ancient stupas dotted the hillside, throwing just enough shade for a worker's noontime nap and for me to sit in comfort and reflect in silence on the history cradled in this valley, feeling a deeper longing to know where Shambhala might be.

~

Heading back east towards Beijing on the railway line that skirts the southern edge of the Gobi Desert, I made a stop at Datong, a filthy coal city west of Beijing and the ancient capital of the Northern Wei people. The Northern Wei artists who built the Yungang grottoes emphasised carving and statuary rather than the delicate murals of the Taklamakan region. I stood stunned at the mouth of the first cave with a big grin on my face as I gazed upon the sculpture before me, delighting in what I saw. It was an extraordinary place. The figures had both an ethereal beauty and a real earthiness, perfectly symbolising the meeting of heaven and earth. Some of the largest figures now looked serenely out to the enormous coal mine across the valley, the front of their caves having collapsed over the years. I glimpsed other giant, tranquil faces behind the mouths of caves cut high in the cliff. In each ground-level cave, former wayside shrines and temples, every inch of wall space seemed to be carved and painted. The large Buddha figures were often recessed, surrounded by hundreds of niches containing symbolic *bodhisattvas* — the great, saintly beings who have vowed to help others achieve buddhahood before themselves — and numerous other buddhas from the past, present and future.

At the front of one cave elephants supported massive

columns, each tier was carved with seated Buddha figures and streams of figures in procession encircled the inner walls, separated by delicate decorative friezes. The wildly decorated ceiling depicted large figures straining out from the top of the wall to 'support' it. Other caves had richly carved pagodas; figures danced and flew, rode elephants, played music and supported the great hand raised in blessing of an enormous Buddha. Hindu influences were evident too, with Shiva seated on a bull and Indra atop an eagle. My heart felt close to bursting. I sat for a long time in front of the monumental seated Buddha of Cave 20, a 14-metre high late fifth-century carving representing the Emperor Wencheng who restored Buddhism to the dynasty after his murderous grandfather persecuted Buddhists and destroyed temples and monasteries. The impassive face, massive shoulders and shallow, stylised drapery showed a strong Central Asian influence although many of the small figures were much more reminiscent of Indian art. It was fascinating, beautiful and inspiring. There were few tourists here. I had time to film at leisure, to sit in the patchy sunlight and draw, happy that at last I had found in abundance examples of the sculpture which had so enticed me in the museum at Shanghai.

Next I headed to Wu Tai Shan, the Buddhist sacred mountain area with the small monastic village of Taihuai at its centre, a day's bus ride from Datong. As my time in

China was drawing to a close, I needed to stop and reflect on the story that was emerging from my experiences over the past month, and I wanted a quiet place to do it. Finding such a place is a challenge in China.

Early the next morning, with the city a dark smudge behind us, our minibus trundled along a quiet country road. From my front seat I saw a huge orange shape come leering towards us. An orange semitrailer, an empty coal truck on its way back to Datong, was passing another of the same colour shape and size. But the country road was not wide enough for the three vehicles, and the semitrailer careened into our bus. Shaving off the entire side of the vehicle, it veered off the road and into a nearby field. Glass flew everywhere and several people in the back of the bus were cut, one woman quite badly, her seat suddenly exposed to the now empty road. In the quiet countryside her screams sounded very loud. My pack and its previously accessible medical kit were in the back, but the back door was pushed in and jammed shut. After some minutes of ineffectual activity a taxi drew up and took the injured woman, the driver and three others into a nearby town.

We waited for four hours in the rain. A police jeep arrived and two policemen measured the road, then climbed back into the jeep and waited. Lots of people stopped to look. In the front of the bus I sang ABC songs to two small boys and attempted to talk with the women. I tried to read and did a little filming. Early in the afternoon a replacement vehicle arrived, with a tool box. We prised open the back door of the bus, transferred my pack to the new bus and set off again towards the mountains. Much later as we climbed up a steep mountain road I heard something go 'clunk', steam poured out of the engine compartment and we pulled onto the side of the road. I had to laugh. Far below us I saw the silvery thread of a mountain stream, 'a good climb for the hapless driver in search of water', I thought, and sat by the side of the road to wait.

The mountains were covered in little fir trees and red and yellow wildflowers. The valley, enclosed by the five sacred mountains, was until recently fairly inaccessible and so escaped the worst of the destruction of the Cultural Revolution. The valley floor is dominated by a large white stupa, and there are over two dozen old temples and monasteries in and around the valley. I spent two days exploring the mountain paths, visiting temples and drawing, drinking in the unpolluted, fir-fragrant air and relishing the silence. One soft evening I chanced across the state-owned Shanxi Provincial Opera Company who were performing on a makeshift stage in a tent, in a vacant lot at the bottom of the main street. And I met David, a French photographer who spoke both English and

Mandarin. He arranged for us to spend time backstage with the opera company members, a cast of sixty with ages ranging from fourteen to sixty-three, the youngest having started when she was eleven. The company tours only the four provinces in which their dialect can be understood for eight months of the year, then rehearses for two months and has two months off, when it's too cold to do anything. Theatre always has an element of magic, but this was different: the costumes, the makeup and especially the music. The music was difficult to understand at first, but by the third performance I had been tucked into the orchestra pit beside a smiling young man who played a stringed instrument I'd never seen before, and was loving every minute of it. Below the stage, the upturned faces of a rapt audience who were squatting on rocks and logs were just about as interesting as the performance itself.

I was finding it difficult to leave this little village and the hospitality of the opera company, but my visa was due to expire. I had only three days before I was booked to leave China by train for Mongolia. Reluctantly, I took a bus to Beijing. The wrong bus as it turned out. Wu Tai Shan was full of touts for the *miandis* (minibuses) because the town is sometimes full of tourists, but locals say they are unreliable and slow, and I knew a public bus ran each morning to Taiyuan where I could pick up a connection to Beijing. It is called the *gong gong chiche*, a good name I thought. But the touts lied: 'No no, that is not, this is public bus.' When I realised I had been tricked, I refused to pay my fare until we reached the public bus station at Taiyuan. '*Bu hao* (not good)!' I said, angry and frustrated.

The minibuses rely on the bus being as full as possible and so stop in every settlement shouting their destination until the required number of people are on board. Sometimes this can take half an hour, and the hustlers shout very loudly. I became angrier and my resistance to each new event, stronger and stronger. I couldn't even watch the scenery or the activity in the streets without seething: 'When will this damn bus fill up and leave!' Around lunchtime as the driver changed a flat tyre, I looked up to see the *gong gong chiche* serenely chugging past, with one passenger. Eventually, obviously sick of my bad temper, they offloaded me onto another *miandi*, insisting that this one was definitely going to the Beijing bus station. It didn't. I finally arrived in steaming, noisy, polluted Beijing with a raging sore throat, taut with tension, feeling very sorry for myself and with compassion for no one.

A Dry Land

I was starting to wonder if I'd done the right thing. It seemed faintly ridiculous to be looking for signs of esoteric knowledge when most of my time and energy was taken up with the endless difficulties of day to day existence within a very different culture to my own — a society that was itself preoccupied with finding its way into the twenty-first century. Just one month into the journey, I'd already travelled several thousand kilometres out to the Tibetan Plateau and back again and had barely set foot in the Kunlun mountains, let alone found mysterious tunnels or flickering lights in the deserts. It seemed a long, long way to Mount Belukha in search of a mythic land. But I was determined to get a feel for these high deserts and plateaux, and circumnavigating the mountain ranges that held them still seemed the best way to do this.

Right now though I couldn't wait to leave Beijing. Having forgotten the guidebook warnings, I'd nearly had my passport withheld by the Public Security Bureau because I hadn't renewed my visa in good time, so it was with a sigh of relief that I settled into my comfortable bunk on the train that was taking me out of China and into Mongolia.

I met Toni and Ana on the train. There were a few tourists in our carriage — this was the Trans-Mongolian Express, and several people were on the first leg of a trip across to Moscow, but Toni, Ana and I were getting off at Ulaan Baatar, the capital of Mongolia. They were a Portuguese couple — he was a travel photographer and she wrote articles for European travel magazines — and like me, they wanted to spend some time in the Gobi Desert, the vast, largely semi-arid zone which covers the southern third of Mongolia.

About three per cent of the Gobi is a 'true' desert of drifting sand, eroded mountains and barren rocky plains, but even here there are occasional oases providing water and good grass for the nomads and their animals. The whole region is alive with wildlife, the reason for Toni and Ana's visit, but I knew there was no public transport into the Gobi, and few roads; we would need a four-wheel-drive vehicle and a driver who was familiar with the maze of jeep tracks that cover the desert, someone who could easily locate a spring or well in the middle of nowhere, someone we could trust in this sparsely populated, isolated region.

At a guesthouse in the middle of Ulaan Baatar, we made the arrangements as quickly as possible. Tsetseg, a woman with many contacts who ran the guesthouse, arranged a 'tour' with a driver who had his own Russian four-wheel-drive van, and a young man who would translate for us. After Beijing's noise, pollution and the constant crush of people I was starting to ache for some wide, open spaces, horizons that visibly followed the curve of the earth, and silence.

Our translator, Sainu, took us shopping in the 'container market' — a large dusty outdoor space tightly lined with shipping containers that had become tiny shops. Sainu was a tutor at the local unversity. Although young, he had the slightly overweight, soft body of a sedentary man. His skin glowed golden, his smile was wide and white and his eyes were beautifully almond-shaped, but he had a slightly impatient manner, leading us around the maze of shops as if it were a chore he'd like to finish as quickly as possible. There were thieves aplenty here, and more than once I felt surreptitious tugs at my daypack, as always in marketplaces, worn on the front of my body. I was starting to sense an underlying depression in this town, like a low-level hum. The buildings had a rather dilapidated, 'Sovietised' look and the huge squares, wide boulevards and ugly apartment blocks reminded me that the Russians had been here until very recently. I knew that some of the nomadic population was drifting into town unable to compete in the recently freed-up marketplace, and a homeless population was growing rapidly. Drunkenness was also a growing problem. One evening as I walked back to the guesthouse, an empty vodka bottle was casually dropped from a third-storey window onto the pavement in front of me, narrowly missing my head. I was happy I didn't have to die on a Mongolian footpath. It was a town of contrasts. A devout Buddhist community keeps the temples active, but every nightclub boasts a strip show, and in the town centre, traditionally dressed men and women rub shoulders with young Mongolians in the latest hip gear; a dress code which seemed to make compulsory, unbelievably high, platform-soled shoes.

Tsetseg took us one night to one of the nightclubs to celebrate a friend's graduation from the university, describing the evening as 'Mongolian music and striptease'. It was a very strange night. Beautiful, sultry Mongolian women moved slowly around the small dance floor to truly awful music, stopping in front of each table to writhe inside their small glittering costumes, pouting and unwilling to make eye contact; couples wildly danced the Twist, and groups formed circles to dance en masse, an opportunity to smile and wiggle at the stranger opposite. Tsetseg's friend sat impassive, sipping at a beer. I didn't know if he was bored, or embarrassed. Late in the evening two women performed a full striptease on the little stage, spreading their legs and rubbing their pubis up and down strategically placed poles, an impersonal rendition of simulated sex that left me feeling slightly self-conscious and a little incredulous that such a cool charade could generate so much excitement, but it sent the clubbers into a wild and frenzied groin-grinding dance. Tsetseg's friend was still unmoved but she was having a very good time, and ordered another strip show, specifically for her friend. The stripper gave up on him after one turn around the dance floor, choosing instead another good-looking member of our party to shake her enormous breasts at. The whole bizarre scene seemed to illustrate graphically the extremes of behaviour that can occur when tight controls are lifted.

At 6.00 am on 15 June, Toni, Ana and I loaded our gear into the Russian van and travelled across town to pick up Sainu. His father and his grandfather were there to see us off — it was Sainu's first trip into the desert, and he was as excited as we were. His grandfather, a small well-preserved eighty-five-year-old, had milk to bless our trip. We each

drank a cup and as we drove off, I turned to see him throw the remainder of the milk after us. It was an auspicious act.

The Gobi has not always been a desert. Many millennia ago a cataclysmic climate change, circa 10,000 BCE according to many geologists, transformed much of Central Asia and Siberia into desert and semi-arid steppe. The Gobi is said to have once been a northern inland sea; and an old Mongolian legend tells of the isle of 'Shambhaling' that lay in this sea, a place where poverty was unknown, gold abounded and the land flowed with milk and honey. This sea may well have drained to become, for some time at least, a lush, fertile and inhabited land — there are also tales of ancient cities lying buried beneath the Gobi sands, exposed sometimes by the fierce winds that sweep across the desert, to be covered over again just as quickly. It's fairly certain that the Uyghur people, some of whom I was to meet months later, once had a great empire on the edge of the Gobi. Momentarily caught up in a romantic, naive fantasy, I thought how wonderful it would be to experience such an archaeological revelation, a lost city unveiled, but fortunately the next two weeks didn't present us with the horrors of a serious sand storm.

Munkhuu was our driver. His name means 'happiness forever' and he truly was a happy man. We spent our first day driving across the steppes of the semi-Gobi, where nomadic horsemen were intent on selecting mounts for the upcoming Naddam Festival races, the biggest social event of the year. It was cloudy and cool with patches of sunshine, and changing patterns of light, shade and colour over the green-brown steppes. A few kilometres out of town we had moved onto the jeep tracks, a confusing crisscrossing of trails that Sainu incomprehensibly called an 'angry road' whenever they intersected. We were headed towards a low line of craggy black mountains on the horizon, over which was poised a small black cloud.

It grew colder and started to rain as we drew close late that afternoon, the mountains rearing out of the soft plains that were still banded with colour. We stopped at a *ger* (the large white felt tent of the nomads), which was tucked into a stony hillside. Munkhuu got lost occasionally and needed to ask directions, but he decided we would stay the night there. We felt shy — even Munkhuu didn't know these people, and the family was large with five children. We were paying guests, but it wasn't obvious how we would all fit into this tent to sleep. The *ger* was circular, the canvas sides with their thick felt inner wall were well fastened down in the cold weather, and the orange poles (the colour of the sun) that made up the collapsible wooden frame were visible at the small opening at the top. The stove at the centre of the *ger* was lit, the smoke struggling through the high opening which had that night been partially covered as the cold rain still fell. The small, brightly painted wooden door, always positioned to face south, was firmly closed against the weather. We sat around the darkening *ger* in silence, a little uncomfortable at first. I was to discover over the next two weeks that these nomadic peoples are not overly talkative and that silence is a natural quality of *ger* life, perhaps a reflection of the vast landscape in which they live and move.

As guests, we had entered the *ger* on the left side, traditionally the male half of the tent, and were now seated towards the back of the *ger*, a place of honour. The area of highest status is the back of the *ger* where the elders sit, and treasured possessions are kept. Here, as in every *ger* I subsequently entered, is the Buddhist altar, with Buddhist images and family photographs prominently displayed. The youngest child, Temje, was seven and was nicknamed Toraa, or 'little pig'. He was a most curious and good-natured boy who wanted to inspect everything we had, several times. I took out my pencil and paper and started to draw him — his sisters were very shy and retreated every time I looked their way. We all started to relax. His mother offered us hot milk tea, yoghurt and hard biscuits called *buursog*, and made a rich dessert as a special treat — cream and flour cooked together forming a paste. It was difficult to eat and I felt nausea rise in my throat as I tried to finish the dish. A vegetarian diet in China had been delicious, fresh and light and utterly unlike anything I had eaten in Chinese restaurants in the West. But here in this landlocked country of roaming herds few vegetables are grown. The soil is frozen for a large part of the year, and anyway, very little grows in the Gobi except for tough grasses and the saxaul bush.

It's often assumed that the Mongols eat nothing but meat, but in summer the nomads give their stomachs some respite by eating what is called 'white food'. All kinds of sour milk, curds and cheeses are made from the milk of the five domesticated animals — cows, camels, horses, goats and sheep. Mare's milk is fermented to produce *airag*, a slightly sparkly, pleasantly acid drink prepared by a method unchanged since the thirteenth century. The milk is collected in a leather bag and simply churned, and as both milk and *airag* symbolise happiness, it's an indispensable part of the meal during celebrations and festivities. Gobi *airag* is appreciated for the special flavour of the desert grasses. They were flavours too subtle for me to discern, but I liked the freshness of the sour, fizzy, slightly alcoholic drink, and I especially liked the milky spirit called *shimmin arkhi* that was distilled from the *airag*. With around twelve per cent alcohol content, a few glasses can produce an intoxication that is light and funny and unlike the drunkenness that comes from imbibing vodka, the drink that was introduced by the Russians. Sainu and Munkhuu liked it too and designed detours to drink the *shimmin arkhi* of celebrated nomad distillers. In one *ger* where I had taken great pains to set up an interview with a nomadic woman, with Sainu as both cameraman and translator, the interview degenerated with each glass of *shimmin arkhi*. Each of my more and more incoherent questions met with greater howls of laughter as the two men rolled around on the carpet holding their aching sides, the woman shaking silently with giggles, her children wide-eyed and mouths agape. The footage was unusable, but very funny.

At about 5.00 pm Sainu suddenly told us it was time to rest. We assumed this meant a very early bedtime, obediently laid our sleeping bags in a row on the carpet to the side of the *ger* and tried to prepare mentally for sleep. But I could hear the children washing dishes, and soon people were quietly talking and three hours later everyone was up again! We went for a walk in the freezing wind. A three-day-old foal stumbled around its mother and suspicious family dogs slunk behind us, growling under their breath, a warning to us not to get too close. A wide band of luminous pale green separated the horizon from the black sky.

Everyone rose early the next morning, the girls to milk goats and cows and the father and his eldest son to check the wellbeing of the animals after the cold night. The foal was still alive and well. I later heard stories of sick and freezing animals being given vodka to kick-start the system but our gift of two bottles obviously wasn't going to end up in the medicine cabinet. After we'd given the children small gifts I sang a farewell song, which had to be toasted before and after, and then everyone else sang, and we drank to each song. 'Summertime' became my favourite thank-you song, as I could so easily change the words to fit the local environs, and I had Sainu to translate for me:

Summertime, and the airag is easy,
Foals are jumping,
And the pasture is high …

It's a great courtesy to wish a nomadic herder 'high pastures', because summertime is the only season they will have them — the winters are long and often desperately harsh, and the lifestyle is simply hard, hard work.

It was still early when we loaded the van and drove off into a clear day, towards the Gobi proper. We were the only traffic. This was to be the pattern of our days in this extraordinary place. Munkhuu was a wonderful driver with a great sense of humour — as dry as the discarded Gobi snakeskins I collected from our picnic spots. When one day three Kulaan (wild ass) were spotted on a stony plain, still some distance from us, he decided that this was an opportunity not to be missed. Toni was intent on photographing as much of the wildlife as could be found, and had already been thwarted in a perfect shot of a gazelle when Sainu leaned out of the van window, pointed an imaginary rifle at the frozen creature and startled it into full flight. It was a childish act and we were all irritated, even Munkhuu, as he'd tried many times to outrun the animals or round them up to get close for our benefit. It seemed an impossibility; they could easily outrun the vehicle, sometimes suddenly veering off across the track right in front of us and then springing off in a completely different direction. But now even Sainu was excited. The large ass has not only dwindled significantly in numbers, it is also very shy of humans and not many Mongolians have ever seen one. The chase that Munkhuu gave was thrilling — especially as small rivulets had carved narrow channels into the desert that were deep enough to break an axle if encountered at some speed, and they were hard to see until we were almost on top of them. We were moving — but so were the asses. They can run at over 60 kilometres per hour, but the stallion with his two mares was just playing with us. As we drew close, only to screech to a halt at yet another mini-ravine, he turned to face us, tossing his long powerful head in a gesture of victory and wheeled to join his mares. His hindquarters were massive, an impressive reminder of his strength and speed. We gave in gracefully, but not before I had caught this magnificent animal for a few seconds on film — a piece of tape that became favourite viewing in many *gers* across the Gobi, and consequently flattened many batteries.

The desert is abundant with wild animals, birds and stunning landscapes. At Yolyn Am inside the National Park called Gobi Gurvan Saichan (The Three Beauties of the Gobi) a small, steep-sided gorge holds compact ice from frozen winter rain, only some of which melts in summer. Above the craggy black cliffs of the gorge circle vultures, which drop bones from a great height to smash them, revealing the edible marrow inside. Argali (wild sheep), with immense curled horns, live in the rocky hills and wild goats live in the higher rocks. We saw a lone sheep on a high hillside, and later, a herd of goats clambering across a cliff face. Munkhuu said he had seen a snow leopard in the cliffs of the gorge, and the rare Gobi bear is said to live there too. We were invited to spend the night in the home of the park ranger, Erdenebelig, a gentle man whose wife was away in a township school teaching, although his two sons lived with him. His two *gers* were tucked into a grassy hillside, and he ran a herd of sheep and goats. It seemed a peaceful spot, but wolves had taken nine of the foals of his eleven mares that had recently given birth. He said wolf numbers had been increasing in the last few years, although he was unable to explain why this was so. Erdenebelig was a woodcarver with a clear discerning eye and steady hand. He carved tiny replicas of the wild animals of this region from a strongly perfumed wood called *arts*, a most apt name I thought, although I did wonder sometimes if I had properly understood Sainu's translations!

Next morning I got up early; my right knee, my hip, my whole right leg had been hurting since I'd started sleeping on the carpeted floors of the *gers*, a deep ache I couldn't relieve with stretching, that aspirin only momentarily dulled. I couldn't stay lying on the hard ground and went out to set up the solar battery charger in the first rays of the sun. Erdenebelig's old dog came with me, friendly and gentle like his owner, and most unlike the majority of the nomads' dogs I met who were surly, suspicious beasts. I'd noticed a fluorescent light and a black and white TV set in the *ger* where Erdenebelig slept with his sons. When I asked Sainu about the power source he said there were underground cables, and he was offended when I told him it was a ridiculous idea. We were, after all, in the middle of over a million square kilometres of nothingness. I was beginning to suspect he often made up answers to avoid having no answer. As I was setting up the charger Erdenebelig came out of his *ger*, grinning broadly, in his hand a set of four small, simple solar panels, Chinese-made with two batteries. He was very interested in the wiring configurations of my set and I realised how perfect these would be for the nomadic lifestyle. Small, lightweight with an unlimited energy source. Before I left the desert I'd had the opportunity to sell my set several times over.

I loved this country. I had not expected the subtle beauty I was finding in the desert, nor had I been aware that such dramatic landscapes existed away from the high mountain ranges. The foothills of the eroded desert mountain range Ich Bogd (The Big Godhead) contain some of the most important fossil sites in the world. Called Bayanzag, the 'flaming cliffs', they consist of red crustaceous sandstone which has eroded into fantastic cliffs and gorges. Munkhuu picked the best time of day to drive us there — sunset, with the rocks glowing deep red, the mountain range a stark purple-black and the desert plains a soft pale green. I couldn't believe how ancient it looked. I had already seen the reconstructed skeletons of the enormous flesh-eating dinosaur the Tarbosaurus and its little cousin, a duck-billed plant-eating creature called Saurolophus (a baby at only 8 metres) at the Museum of Natural History in Ulaan Baatar before we came down; and the tiny local museum was full of fossilised dinosaur eggs and sundry bones. But the eerie beauty of this place suddenly put the museum pieces into context. I would have happily camped in the shadow of the cliffs and stayed for days but Munkhuu had found friends in a nearby *ger*. We would stay the night with them.

Munkhuu's friends were a young, recently married couple. Sainu told me that local marriages break up fairly regularly, and that Mongolians are pretty relaxed about sex and marriage. This couple appeared very happy with their new status, loving and comfortable with each other, and it didn't feel intrusive to be staying in their sparsely furnished *ger*. But Sainu, without asking, had been offering my services as a portrait artist (blithely unaware it was not my strong point) and tonight was no exception. The offer was always made to the male head of the family, in this case a handsome young man with fine features. Sainu had no idea that drawing after a couple of aspirin (for my now constantly sore knee and hip) and a few shots of vodka would be problematic for me in that it would take me off the boil, artistically speaking. My heart sank as I pulled out pencil and paper; it would have been discourteous to refuse to draw, but I could barely focus my eyes with the combination of desert sun and the drugs. Sure enough, it was a bad drawing. The young man looked at it in silence for a few moments then spoke briefly to Sainu. I insisted he translate. Reluctantly he told me what I was expecting to hear — the young man disliked the drawing saying it was 'not good'.

Things went from bad to worse. Until now Sainu had been doing his job and alerting the women to my non-meat diet, generally not a problem as so much 'white food' was available, together with rice and homemade noodles; but tonight, unsettled by the drawing incident and fuelled by too much vodka, he had obviously forgotten. I tried to pick out the bits of meat as unobtrusively as possible, palming them and planning to quietly dispose of them later. Toni and Ana had done the same. Although the dry noodle dish was very tasty, they had been unable to successfully chew the hard dry meat. Toni offered to throw mine out too into the desert darkness. Sainu, who had been watching us, told me it was an insulting thing to do, and spoke to our hosts. I felt terrible, embarrassed and ashamed, and very angry with Sainu. More vodka came out as friends from neighbouring *gers* arrived, and jokes were made about the Australian. I didn't need to understand the language to know what the sideways looks, the laughter and the word 'Australian' added up to. Ana was irate too. Although we were paying him a good wage regardless of his inexperience, our guide had become progressively complacent and lazy. We resolved to speak with him the following day. Sleep was impossible for hours, the floor was very hard, and two of the male guests smoked; the conversations were loud and music played throughout the night. The last guest left at 3.00 am and at 6.00 am a man arrived on a motorbike, apparently parking it right beside my head. I felt tired, grumpy and already very hot. At our first stop on the day's drive, trying to keep a neutral, even voice, I told Sainu why I was upset with his behaviour. He threw a tantrum, sulked like a small child and didn't speak to us for two days.

We drove for long hours across the desert, stopping at lunchtime to picnic — sometimes in a totally featureless landscape with just the shade thrown by the van to keep off the noonday sun. One minute there would be no one on a 360-degree horizon — minutes later visitors would arrive, on horseback or by motorbike, to share lunch or just to have a chat and a cigarette, and a cup of tea. It was a chance for Munkhuu to gather information, to find out who had moved on to summer feeding grounds, and which well they were relying on for their water. We were equally reliant on these wells, as was every other large living creature. When drawing water it was mandatory to put some out for the animals, even though there may not be a four-legged creature in sight. Perhaps they could smell the water, or it may simply have been our presence at the well, but before you could drag up the second bucket there would be an unruly queue waiting for a sip. Occasionally, if more than one stallion had brought his mares in, the unruliness turned to bloody biting and kicking with no holds barred. Sadly, the water level of some wells was so low it was impossible to reach a bucket down, and we were compelled to move on to the next well leaving an expectant crowd of animals with their thirst unslaked.

At the southern edge of the national park lie the great sand dunes of Chongoryn Els, the 'singing sands'. At a height of about 800 metres, they run for 100 kilometres along the edge of a wide stony valley and in some places are up to 20 kilometres wide. Rising abruptly behind them, a jagged range of purple-black mountains provides the perfect colour and textural contrast to the soft yellow sand of the massive dunes. No one had been able to explain to me why they were called 'singing sands'. Ana and I had laboriously climbed the highest ridge, battling a shrieking wind and flying sand to experience the view of the desert in the evening light. All we could hear was the howl of the wind. The whiplash of sand made it impossible to take the camera out, so we turned tail and followed our rapidly disappearing footsteps back down the ridges and across the sweeping hollows of sand, only to be stopped short by an extraordinary sound. It was low, deep and resonant, as if a disembodied voice was calling from the ether. It didn't seem to be related to the sand — it came from everywhere and nowhere. It was the primordial sound, *Aum* (*Om*), and I was transfixed. Now I understood why no one had been able to describe the sound.

At the northern end of the valley a small river seeps between low sandhills, providing some welcome green in the otherwise dry landscape. Sainu solemnly warned us not to wash in this river — it was poisonous, he said, and our skin would drop off. Here we stayed with Aldarmaa, a woman with three children, a large tabby cat which silently slid in and out of the *ger* under the bottom flaps of the tent — the only cat I saw in Mongolia — and large herds of goats, sheep and horses. I asked her if she found it difficult to look after a family and the herds on her own. 'No,' she said, 'I have my son to help me, he's a good boy.' The thirteen-year-old boy gave a huge shy smile. Wherever we went I saw that it was the children in these nomads' camps who expressed the special qualities of this remarkable region. They were tough but beautiful. They worked very hard for long hours, but were able to give themselves over wholeheartedly to play with an engaging freshness and joy. It was comparatively easy for me to show through the camera's eye the qualities and colours of the landscape, and to capture something of the life of these people. I wished, however, that I could show the spontaneous moments when the children suddenly lost their shyness and wanted to play, or the times when the jokes started to flow with the *airag*. It was impossible to foresee all these film-worthy moments, particularly without the threads of language to alert me to possibilities; but sometimes it felt good simply to be a participant.

After having spent a comfortable night at the oasis, cuddled up to the cat snuggled between sleeping bags, I went out for a walk at sunrise. Aldarmaa and the children were already up attending to animals, preparing for milking and getting the fire lit for breakfast. There are no trees in the Gobi so the fires are fuelled with animal dung, a fuel that gives off a good heat. There had been five children in the *ger* that night, as Aldarmaa was looking after her sister's two, and suddenly as I rounded the *ger*, it was all on for a game of monsters, with me as the mighty wrestling monster. Why me? I was the biggest, and without language a monster can get by with a lot of heavy-duty grunting. It was as though a signal had been given for the shyness to be dropped and the fun to begin.

We were heading north now, almost on the last leg of the long drive back to Ulaan Baatar. Sam and Tumna were two dazzling seven-year-olds who lived at another oasis beside a fast-flowing river at the site of a sacked monastery, one of many monasteries destroyed in the 1930s. Thousands of monks had been arrested and murdered during Stalinist-inspired purges, in a campaign against religion that saw the ransacking, closure or burning of more than 700 monasteries and the disappearance of an estimated 17,000 monks of middle and high rank. Henning Haslund, who spent over three years with Sven Hedin's Central Asiatic Expeditions in 1927–1930, had this to say about the early purges:

> We heard that in Outer Mongolia the Red Soviet was more and more extending its power, that the lamas had been called up to the army, that high taxes had been laid on the people and that everywhere a

> 'new freedom' prevailed which the Mongols failed to understand. The highest representatives of the land … had been driven out, and so had many of their religious leaders. Some had been killed or thrown into prison, others put in irons and sent away to degrading forced labour in Urga.[4]

In 1937 the slaughter and pillage began in earnest, and it was only in 1990 that freedom of religious worship was restored. This particular monastery had been a large one, spread over a grassy flat above the river in a pretty little valley lined with trees, the first we had seen in nearly two weeks. It was easy to imagine it as a thriving religious community in a small garden of Eden tucked into the desert. The river water was clear, the bottom was sandy — there seemed no danger of my skin dropping off this time. After I'd washed most of my clothes and floated down the river on the current for a satisfying time I decided to go for a walk to explore the ruins. It was nearly evening — I was enchanted by the light the desert produces at this time. I felt the two little figures come up behind me before I saw them, without a word they slipped their hands into mine and beamed up at me. Their candour and warmth were irresistible — they were going to be my guides to the monastery.

Next morning Sam and Tumna were at the camp

early. They'd brought along two nine-year-old friends, Lobsaa and Rant. The girls wore huge bows of gauzy fluorescent material in their hair, rainbows of colour over jet-black hair that didn't budge one centimetre during the children's leaps and whirls, and even stayed firmly in place during the long swims that were accompanied by much shrieking and splashing. It was a wondrously happy group of children. They seemed to find humour and joy in just about everything they did. Theirs was a world devoid of most of the trappings that Western children take for granted, and in this remote area they were probably little touched by the changes and instability that are beginning to affect Ulaan Baatar. There was a 'centredness' about the way they lived their lives in this verdant oasis.

There was a definite sense of freedom about being in this landscape. It was vast, totally absorbing, and I felt serenely happy in its stillness and silence — a silence without edges. While watching a big group of baby camels leaping and bouncing across the sand early one morning, our last in the desert, I was reminded of the energy of the children we'd met in the river valley, their acceptance of the hardworking life they led and the joy they took in their play. I wrote daily in my journal, photographed the ever-changing landscape, and filmed a story that was beginning to make sense to me.

But back in Ulaan Baatar, shattering news awaited

me. My eighty-two-year-old mother, who had been so excited about this journey, pinning maps marked with my route onto her kitchen wall — had unexpectedly but peacefully died. It was so strange, to be told of her death in the telephone box at the Ulaan Baatar post office. I cried my eyes out while people watched, curious, and a young man who sold paintings generously helped me feed coins into the slot. I knew my mother was getting ready to die — I just didn't think I would be in Mongolia when it happened. My family were adamant — the funeral would be postponed if I wanted to return, and I was suddenly faced with a painful decision — whether to abandon my journey and return home, or keep moving on.

Before I left for the desert I had spent several hours at one of the large monasteries in Ulaan Baatar, soaking up the peace and solitude and watching the locals come and go from the temples, so when Sainu arrived next morning to take me to see the Head Lama of his local temple, our differences made redundant by this new event, it was a comfortable decision. He was adamant that the 'opening of the golden casket' was the only way to ritualise my mother's death, and I badly needed a ritual. I knew I could say goodbye from here as easily as anywhere, if 'easily' is the word, and I let Sainu take charge.

We walked up to the cluster of temples, *ger*-shaped buildings with golden roofs. From the Head Lama, a serene man who spoke a little English, I learned that certain 'books' would be read that pertained to my mother's and my linked karmic journeys, and that the monks would chant them the following day to ensure her safe and happy journey from this world. I made an offering of some money, receiving butter candles and incense sticks that I lit in the temple, and some powdered incense and cleansing water to use for my own ritual. I decided to perform my ritual at Terelj, a long alpine valley about 80 kilometres from Ulaan Baatar, and Sainu would drive me there.

The *Tibetan Book of Living and Dying* teaches that a person who has just died should be surrounded with loving and helpful thoughts during the first stages of the *bardo*, the afterdeath state of existence, without allowing emotional attachment to interfere with their process.[5] I'd forgotten to ask when exactly my mother had died, and anyway I was in no state to work out what time it might have been in Mongolia, nor could I remember how long this state of existence, if it existed at all, lasted. I remembered how my father died in his bed at home, in a coma but with his favourite music playing and his family gathered around. I had felt a palpable energy of release at the moment of his death. Was it the same for my mother? Why was I initiating a ritual that made no sense to me intellectually — did I really believe that in burning incense and throwing some water around I could help

Mum on her journey, whatever and wherever that might be? It seemed impossible to do any of this without feeling a strong emotional attachment.

The valley of conifer forest and meadow was filled with wildflowers, and in the narrowest part there was a ridge of enormous rounded rocks that towered above the trees. I asked Sainu to drop me off in one of the meadows — I wanted to walk until I found the right spot. It was a lovely sunny day with bright white scudding clouds. A myriad of insects, audible in the silence of the valley, were buzzing around the flower-filled meadows. Behind me a cuckoo called. Ahead of me another answered it, and I looked up to see a cluster of huge boulders high on the ridge. They resembled the head, shoulders and hands of a woman bent forward in supplication — hands clasped in prayer. I smiled in recognition — Mum had always loved the shining cuckoos at home, and I was willing to believe she was telling me where to have this ritual. It was perfect. It was also very high but I've always loved scrambling around the mountains, and she knew that too.

At the base of the 'hands' was a gentle rock platform, and in a sheltered ring of rocks I burned the incense and wished my mother a safe and happy journey, and sprinkled the water the monks had given me. Perhaps she now knew more about Shambhala that I could ever hope to discover in this lifetime. I remembered the baby camels I'd watched in the desert. The previous evening they'd been tied onto a long line staked in the sand, waiting for their mothers to come back from the desert to feed them. They cried like infant humans as they waited, tears welling up in their eyes, yet the next morning they were leaping and bounding across the sandy expanses as if their mothers had never existed. I thought about mothers letting go of their children, and children letting go of their mothers. Mum had recently admitted she lived for her children but now she'd left us, and I had to deal with the emotional attachment our long relationship had given rise to. I filmed my ritual, hesitantly, the soundtrack punctuated by sniffs and sobs, wondering if people would think I was using my grief for commercial gain, but it seemed important to record these moments.

I sat for a long time on the rocks, looking down into the quiet valley, reflecting on this most unusual journey I was undertaking. I had resolved to continue as planned, spending another four months in the remote interior of Central Asia, on a journey that many people viewed as extreme risk-taking although it seldom felt like that to me. I could die at any time — here or anywhere for that matter. I asked myself whether I would die well, just as my mother had wanted to? According to the Buddhist teachings I must first learn to live well — if I wanted a peaceful death I must first cultivate peace in my mind and learn to be less reactive in difficult situations. For instance, if the Chinese minibus driver who told me lies had crashed into a big orange truck I might have died angry and resentful. This was something to think about.

A Clear Eye in a Dark Forest

At the beginning of July I was on a train again, en route to southern Siberia. I felt miserable, tired and emotionally drained. It was hard making the journey alone now. My goal was to reach the remote national parks of Lake Baikal, although I had no idea how I was going to get there. Clearing customs at the Russian border was a relaxed affair though — a joke about kangaroos and I was through. Then we moved sedately through the *taiga*, the seemingly endless coniferous forests of eastern Russia, to the city of Irkutsk, sitting on the southern shores of Lake Baikal. I'd often wondered what the *taiga* looked like.

In New Zealand our family has a holiday shack on

the western shores of Golden Bay, close to Farewell Spit where thousands of migrating bar-tailed godwits gather at the end of every summer before setting off on their long and perilous journey to Siberia. As a teenager I would sit quietly, watching the numbers of birds grow rapidly each day, and contemplate the journey they were about to take. Did they have any memory of the vast oceans they were preparing to navigate? Did they recognise the *taiga* with its giant trees and deep silence, and know where it ended and the tundra began? The *taiga* of Siberia is largely untouched by the human hand, and with over twenty per cent of the world's standing forests, it provides a habitat for a wondrous array of animals like the Siberian tiger, the brown bear and the Amur leopard (in the north), and wolves. I thought there couldn't be too many places like this left on the planet, where humans live with the threat of danger from animals with which they share their environment. In the misty rain the *taiga* looked dark, mysterious and uninviting. Small villages next to the railway line seemed to huddle protectively in towards their centres, in case the forest got too close; and it was difficult to see more than a few metres into the closely aligned trees. In my miserable state the train seemed a very safe haven.

Irkutsk, on the River Angara, is a modern, pleasant city that still retains a few small suburbs of old wooden houses — many with carved and brightly painted window surrounds that were like winks of light against the dark wood, some that were slowly being reclaimed by the earth as they slid gently into the damp soil, their walls and rooflines tilting at an alarming angle. They must have been very cold in winter, but there was a softness and simplicity to this architecture that sat well against the surrounding *taiga*. In its heyday Irkutsk was referred to as the Paris of Siberia, but my heart just wasn't in city attractions, and I felt aimless. At the guesthouse I discovered that a local bus made the long journey to Olkhon Island on the western side of the lake, and that a hydrofoil had just started a summer timetable, which took it from Olkhon Island to Ust Barguzin on the eastern shore. This settlement abutted the Ust Barguzin National Park that had just been accorded World Heritage status.

The next morning I was at the bus station. The woman in the queue with the backpack was Russian, and Irkutsk was her hometown. She spoke excellent English, in fact she taught English at the university, and was also trying to buy a ticket to Olkhon Island. Tatyana planned to meet friends from Moscow who were camping with a big group of school children, city kids who were having their first big 'outdoors' experience, although she didn't know exactly where on the island they were. She offered to share her tent with me, as neither she nor I knew if there was any other place to stay, and with her help I bought my ticket. Unfortunately it was the last ticket — the bus was very full. 'Don't worry,' she said, 'you will see me later, on the same bus.' I puzzled over this as we pulled out of the bus station and I waved goodbye to her, upset that I had so suddenly lost the opportunity for good company and conversation, and guaranteed shelter for the night. About twenty minutes out of town we were stopped by police; they were checking the buses for overloading and ordered a ticket inspection. A few hundred metres on, around a couple of bends in the road, we stopped again where a white jeep was parked on the roadside. The doors of the bus opened and in climbed Tatyana and two other people.

I was very pleased to see her! Bags were moved around and the newcomers soon had comfortable seats in the aisle, the driver totally unperturbed at the overt flaunting of police regulations, and an obvious party to this ruse. He was more concerned with a large group of university law students at the back of the bus. They were starting their summer holidays and were planning to camp on the lakeshore, fortified by numerous bottles of vodka and beer. Sensibly, they reasoned that if most of the beer was consumed on the bus trip the weight of their bags would be manageable. This led to uninhibited singing, loud card games and an increasingly frustrated bus driver as toilet stops became more and more frequent. Fortunately the vehicle ferry to the island was late; it had run out of petrol.

Lake Baikal was everything I had dreamed of. It's the world's deepest and oldest lake. It is 25 million years old, and filled above two tectonic plates which are moving apart at about two or three centimetres a year, so the sediment in its depths is warm, creating currents and warming the lake in winter — though the top of the lake is frozen thick enough in winter for vehicles to cross. Strange creatures exist in the depths of the lake. In fact over eighty per cent of the fauna is native to this particular lake, and more than 1500 different species of fauna have been identified so far, including a freshwater seal called the Nerpa. Lake Baikal has exceptionally pure water — I don't remember having walked down to a lakeside, to cup my hands and drink from the water lapping into the shore, since I was a child in New Zealand. The serpent in this paradise is industrial pollution, the greatest impact stems from the pulp and paper mill on the southern shore. The Russians would have been hard-pressed to choose a worse industry to place on the shores of Lake Baikal. In 1999 the plant's effluent was equivalent to that from a city of half a million people. Although UNESCO added Baikal to its World Heritage list in 1996, progress towards minimising pollutants has been meagre. Fortunately, I was well away from the southern shore of the lake and it was like a paradise, albeit a cool one.

The men I could see working on the fishing boats at

the wharf were Buryats, the native people of this high mountain steppe country. Legend has it that a mythological ancestor of the Buryats, Great Father Eagle, lived in the mountains of Olkhon Island. He was sent by the gods to protect people from diseases, hunger and misery, but the people didn't trust him so the gods allowed him to marry a woman. The first shaman was born of this marriage. A shaman, making use of various ecstatic spiritual practices, calls upon the hidden powers of the universe to heal the physical and mental diseases of his or her tribespeople, as well as guiding them in matters of the afterlife. The legends say shamans could fly because they were born from the eagle, ascending the World Tree — the Tree of Life of the Biblical Garden of Eden story — in astral flight. In her book *Shambhala*, Victoria Le Page proposes that the Tree of Life has its source in Central Asia.

> The Garden of Eden myth originated in remote times in the region of the Siberian shaman's World Tree, being later carried to every part of the world, and … Shambhala was in fact the first sacred garden.[6]

Was I standing in it?

I walked up onto a bluff as we waited for the ferry to arrive from the island. The slope was covered with tiny wildflowers, deep green mosses and pale lichens. Clouds cast shadows on the surface of the lake. I was reminded of the delicate interplay of light and colour that I'd found so fascinating on the steppes and deserts of Mongolia. Looking down from the bluff into the clear aquamarine water I thought how lucky I was to be standing here in this far-off place, feeling more comfortable every day with the expanding nature of my journey and the story I wanted to tell. My grief was more centred, my thoughts less scattered, as if my mind and my body had received a little nourishment from the rituals I performed after my mother's death. At last I felt a lift in my spirits which seemed connected to this beautiful place.

When the ferry finally arrived there were arguments about who would board first, between the drivers who couldn't back their vehicles onto the deck, and the drunken locals, two of whom were on our bus huffing vodka breath into my face as they swayed in the aisle and took a close look at the foreigner. Eventually the bus arrived at the island's only village where we found Nikita's Place, the only guesthouse. Nikita had not seen the school group from Moscow, but Nikita's friend Anatoly had a four-wheel-drive vehicle and he drove us up the northern shore of the island to look for them in the sand dunes. Evening was drawing close when we found them. A big fire was strung with blackened tin cans as the evening meal was prepared

— gritty rice stew, tea and bread. Wishing Anatoly farewell and thank you, we settled in under the fir trees for the night. I was a long way north — the twilight lasted for hours, the sky slowly sank into the lake, its reflected colours were like 'Colour Field' paintings. It was to be the group's last night on the island — they had moved camp about five times and were by now adept at setting up camp, fire and food. The teachers had brought the group here from Moscow to learn outdoor and cultural skills training. I was told that adults in Russia are steadfastly resisting change, that a staggering eighteen per cent want the Tsar back, and that the youth of Russia is seen as its only salvation. The young people in this group were articulate and delightful. After dark a guitar came out and at midnight I 'hit the sack', for once sleeping well on the hard ground.

Tatyana moved on with the group next day, but I wished she were staying. Apart from speaking English well, she was good company and seemed to intuitively know what I was trying to achieve on this journey. She'd filmed me, very competently, walking onto the ferry and at the rail, watching local men scan the water for schools of *omul* (the main edible fish of Lake Baikal) and we'd spent an hour of our ferry-waiting time in the bus in easy conversation, sharing thoughts on life and living as though we'd known each other forever. I showed her my journal and told her about my mother's death, fighting back tears that welled up whenever I thought about it. She looked through the journal intently then sat up very straight, eyes wide. 'You must write a book,' she said firmly. She asked me, 'What do you think is the reason for this delay — you didn't show me the journal before, or tell me about your mother? The reason is, I was supposed to see this book, and I think you could write a book on your return to Australia. Some people will see the film, but many more will read your book.' As we said goodbye at the village next day she reiterated, 'Please write a book.'

I made Nikita's place my base. Nikita was a tall, blonde, quiet and softly-spoken man. He gave me a steep-ceilinged room upstairs with a front view across the lake to the mountains on the opposite shore and a side-window view of the village. In front of the last row of houses, a steep hill rose up to a bluff above the lake. The sun streamed in through grimy windows. Below me a group of young Russian boys on holiday played noisy war games around an abandoned car using antlers for guns. My bed was set low and comfortable in an alcove in the wall. Locally woven cloths hung from the top of it and were tied to the sides. It was a snug, safe place to sleep. I had three delicious meals a day, every one of which contained fish. For the first time on this trip I gave up any notion of sticking rigidly to a vegetarian diet and ate what I was given — fish dumpling soups, potato fritters with fish, freshly baked bread with homemade cottage cheese, and more fish in every conceivable culinary variation. After the limited diet of Mongolia this was bliss and I ate enthusiastically. The village, forty per cent Buryat and sixty per cent Russian, was spread out over a sandy flat, backed by the forest that covered the rest of the island. The unpainted steep-roofed houses were timber and were sometimes separated by low, timber-paling fences. Groups of dogs roamed the sandy streets. Unlike the Mongolian dogs these were mostly friendly, and all but the oldest were willing to be taken for a walk along the lakeside at the drop of a stick — or rather, many of them took me for walks, running like crazy, happy and almost dizzy with joy it seemed. I walked, also happy.

I explored the island over the next few days. The roads were mainly tracks over sandhills, but Anatoly's Russian jeep was available for longer trips. Olkhon is the biggest island on Lake Baikal — over 70 kilometres long. On its southern side sheer cliffs descend to the deepest part of the lake, which is more than a kilometre and a half deep. The Buryats have numerous legends about spirits and sacred sites around Baikal, believing Olkhon Island to be a centre of spiritual power. On the northern tip of the island, its sacred capes rise majestically out of the water like towering guardians. They were covered with a profusion of beautiful wildflowers — stately thistles, purple and yellow daisies, tiny forget-me-nots and the same strongly scented red lilies that I had seen before in the valley of Terelj in Mongolia, where I had said goodbye to my mother. She had grown forget-me-nots in her garden in New Zealand. There were strong-scented herbs, ice plants and brightly coloured lichens, and pale green conifers with startling orange nuts. A cave at the base of Cape Burchan, named after the Buryats' primary god and considered a sacred shamanistic place by the indigenous people, is now also inscribed with Buddhist prayers since the arrival of Tibetan Buddhism in this area. Buddhism only partially replaced the native shamanistic traditions however — it seems that many people, although not religious in a conventional sense, have a deep love for the cosmology of the Baikal area. Above the shaman's cave on the headland I sat and listened to a group of people singing songs to the lake; and at Buryat shrines, three poles set upright in the earth, offerings were regularly placed — many of them beer and vodka bottles. As in Mongolia, a blessing is invoked by flicking a drop of the alcohol to the earth and heavenwards before drinking, and as it would be insulting to take away any of the gift that is offered, the whole bottle has to be drunk there and then, and the empty bottle laid at the shrines. Broken glass surrounded the shrines and although Anatoly said it was a problem, no one seemed concerned enough to remove it.

This place had a good feeling. The isolation seemed to give people a strong sense of community, demonstrated by the evenings around the fire in the yard at Nikita's where I met a modern-day shaman, Valentin, a Buryat man with two thumbs on his right hand. He said all shamans have a physical sign indicating their calling, and this was his. He talked about the ancient Buryat culture and the relationship of the Buryat people to this land, and about the 'power centres' of the region. The fact that I was standing on one of these didn't surprise me in the least. My original intention, to see if places that have been given great spiritual significance might in some way inform my own inner journey (if I was open and attentive), was unfolding. I resolved to be open to each new experience, to let it play out lightly without forcing it or judging it. Having tried to manipulate situations before (as I had in China), with abysmal results, I knew that doing this would be a kindness to myself but, as is often the way, I would have to be prepared for a couple of steps backwards before the next step forward.

Valentin agreed to be interviewed, as long as we sat on the headland in front of my room so that we could look across to Shaman's Rock, a large and attractive rock which jutted out from a small peninsula further around the lake. I needed a translator, but Nikita's English was not good enough so I asked Christina, a seventeen-year-old holiday-maker who was staying at the guesthouse. She was horrified at the proposed time for the interview — 7.30 the next morning — but reluctantly agreed. I was very excited! This was exactly what I needed for my film, a genuine shaman who could talk about Shambhala. I couldn't believe my good fortune.

In my excitement I lost my focus. Where was the spacious awareness I'd resolved to develop? My strong desire for a unique interview narrowed my thinking, my expectations put a hermetic seal around this single goal and I lost all clarity. I bungled the sound, forgot to take stills pictures, didn't ask about Shambhala and ran out of tape as Valentin talked on and on. He was an educator but in my present frame of mind, he seemed more showman than shaman. Christina, bored and tired, wanted to go back to bed and sleep off her hangover. At least the images were beautiful; I had remembered to compose the shots.

By 7.30 on Wednesday evening I was sitting in the sand at the base of Shaman's Rock waiting for the hydrofoil to arrive to take me across the lake to Ust Barguzin, the nearest town to the national park. From the back deck of the boat there was a clear view of the sacred mountain that plunges into the deepest part of the lake, and of the capes that crested like a bow-wave on the northern tip of the island. At about 10.30 that night, the sun still had not set when the hydrofoil pulled into the wharf at Ust

Barguzin. The wharf looked quite a walk from where I imagined the town to be, but I asked directions to a hotel listed in the guidebook, the Gastinitsa Baikal (my Russian had by now extended into intelligible phrases), and received a friendly arm gesture in a very general direction. Most people seemed to have been met — in cars. Walking down the dirt road away from the wharf I was passed by a Russian van, perhaps a bus, that almost stopped, and then a newish jeep with two young men inside drew up. I thought they were going to drive off again when I used my halting Russian, laughing and shaking their heads, but they piled my pack into the back and I climbed in. They seemed friendly enough and at this time of night I didn't want to be walking (or limping) through the deserted streets of a strange town. I didn't even have a map. In Mongolia I had been told that the man to seek out to get into the national park was called Sasha. Both these men were called Sasha.

Eventually we found the Hotel Baikal, a long, low building set under trees. There were no lights showing, and a large padlock secured the door. There was no other hotel. I asked them if they knew 'Sasha Turist?' and after some head-scratching their faces lit up. The dark-haired driver said, 'Yes, we'll go there, after we've called in to Sasha's place, perhaps you can stay at his parents' house.' Eventually after arrangements were made, we arrived at the home of

'Sasha Turist'. He was not home, but his wife suggested we go straight to the parents' house, and he would visit us there at 11.30 pm. Things were getting complicated and I wasn't following the conversations at all well, but the men were lovely and I was very happy to be organised. We arrived at the parents' large wooden bungalow where an enormous, flourishing vegetable garden filled all the available open space. The rest of the family was waiting for us — Sasha I's wife and his beautiful sister Natasha, married to Sasha II. They were both blonde, beautiful and openly welcoming, and the parents were an utter delight. I had arrived in paradise again. I was given a tiny room in the house, but across a small courtyard was the real family hub, another kitchen with a *banya* (a wood-fired sauna) in a small room to the side. There was no running water in the house so we washed under a tap in the garden while a fire was stoked in the *banya* for me. The mother was an excellent cook, who offered much more food than I could possibly finish without feeling ill. A bottle of vodka was produced to go with the meal, perhaps to slow up the eating (I hoped) and I was observed closely by the father as the first toast was made. Was the Westerner up to it? Little did he know his guest was a winemaker's daughter. I made a toast to family hospitality but they were horrified! They thought I'd said 'hospital', but fortunately Natasha spoke a little English and I was forgiven.

At 11.30 Sasha III arrived. He was an extraordinarily good-looking man (Siberia seemed to be full of such handsome men), he was the head ranger of the national park, and yes he was going into the park tomorrow with a UNESCO conference. Would I like to come too? The conference had a day trip on a barge organised, but he could arrange for me to stay inside the park if I wished. We adjourned to the house of a translator for ten minutes to sort out the logistics. I would pay Sasha III for transport in and out of the park, spend the day with the group, then stay at the barge 'hotel'. I would be picked up on Saturday, stay with the family on Saturday night, take the bus to Ulaan Ude on Sunday and catch my train on Monday. And it was okay to film the UNESCO conference. I was delighted — it couldn't have turned out better. Back with the family I had a *banya*, looked at Natasha and Sasha's wedding photos, and tried to sleep.

The UNESCO group was mainly Russian from this and other Russian national parks, and Greenpeace representatives from Moscow; but it also included a couple from a Newfoundland national park, and four Americans, two of whom managed the Florida Everglades National Park. The conference had been convened to explore ways in which the delicate balance of the lake's ecosystem could be maintained with the expected influx of visitors that comes when World Heritage status is granted to an area. The conference would also ascertain what benefits would be accrued with the international attention that would inevitably be focused on the park. One of the visiting scientists, an ecosystem specialist, told me it was imperative the local community be intimately involved in the management of the park. After all, the Buryat people were offering their backyard to the world and contributing to what is so special about Lake Baikal and its environs — a unique, utilitarian culture with strong values attached to the land and the water.

A small barge pulled us over the river, a convoy of jeeps and trucks then drove slowly across to the Svyatoy Nos (Holy Nose) peninsula that juts dramatically out into the lake like a crooked beak (another sacred area for the indigenous Buryat people) and into the Zabaikal National Park. I was told there were bears in the steep, deeply forested hills and rocky peaks of the peninsula, but they were obviously staying well away. The meeting that day was held on the sandy beach of an idyllic bay to which we were taken by Park patrol boats. Lunch was served on long tables arranged on a grassy flat above the beach. The waiters were muscular park rangers wearing jungle greens and striped singlets. The sun shone, the water lapped, dark blue against the white sand, and the translators spoke English. Was this how one achieved transcendence? All I needed now was my bed for the night.

Later that afternoon the meeting adjourned for informal talks to a bay where hot springs bubbled up beside the lake's edge, and there Sasha showed me to my accommodation for the next few days — an old houseboat moored next to a sand spit with the lake on one side and the virgin *taiga* forest on the other.

I spent long periods in my tiny room overlooking the water, watching the changing patterns of light and the easy flow of traffic outside my window — the boats of local fishermen putt-putting across the bay, occasionally pulling in to the houseboat, and taking off again loaded with bottles of vodka. The food couldn't have been fresher. As I had done on Olkhon Island I ate delicious fresh fish (*riba*) for breakfast, lunch and dinner. The houseboat even had its own little *banya* and a generator powered the heaters, stoves and hot-water showers. I spent hours keeping company with Victor, the houseboat's maintenance man, learning Russian and teaching him English. There were three hot springs on the beach, one a searing 60°C, the others pleasantly warm and only big enough to accommodate three or four people. I baulked, however, at the cold water plunge into the lake that northerners insist is so beneficial for the body after the heat of a sauna or hot springs bath. I was content to make paddleboat trips around the large bay. One day at the beach a soldier called Kazanzec, who was camped across the water on a fishing holiday, handed me a small but exquisitely patterned green grass snake with orange flashes above its eyes. It calmly twisted around my arm and slithered across my body, its tongue flicking like crazy. It was not poisonous, I was told. The snake felt nice to hold, but I was glad it wasn't any bigger.

The same day Victor and Kazanzec took me down to the birch forest at the end of the bay in the paddleboat to gather food for dinner. They paddled, I sat. Kazanzec was a man of great enthusiasm for life, full of energy and delight in the natural world. It was hard for me to imagine him as a soldier. He was more like the bull in a story I used to read to my daughter — Ferdinand, who for all his great size and strength would much rather stay in his field and smell the flowers than fight in the bullrings. We stopped at mineral springs to drink. Kazanzec leapt out before the boat stopped to go over to the bank where the spring leaked into the lake. We gathered wild thyme for *chai* (tea), picked a tiny white insignificant flower from which, Victor told me, eau de cologne is made, and gathered huge bundles of a slim green leaf with a slightly peppery flavour that I understood was wild garlic. This was pristine wilderness — Mother Earth at her most beneficent. The air under the birch trees was thick with huge mosquitoes, but this was also tick country. In Mongolia, the people who had told me about Sasha had left one of their party in hospital in

Irkutsk, infected by a tick, which apparently can cause encephalitis. I wasn't taking any chances. I wore a hat, long sleeves and trousers, and I slathered every inch of exposed flesh in repellent. Kazanzec was shirtless, casually swatting mosquitoes as he worked — a tough man who wanted me to try everything that was edible in this forest! Back at the houseboat the cook, Galina, took the greens and made them into a salad with hardboiled eggs and mayonnaise. It was so delicious I ate far too much, and paid for it the next day.

I dreamed I was with a man who taught me to jump into deep water from a great height, without fear. Somehow sex was in there too, but I just remember the jumping, feet first, straight as a die. No fear. I liked lying in bed, listening to the noises of the boat and the people, the sun streaming in, but this was my last day on the houseboat. I didn't want to leave. When I thought of my imminent departure, a fist clenched around my heart and tears came to my eyes. I sat in the sun on the stern deck writing my journal, trying to avoid the attentions of a local fisherman who'd had far too much vodka — a nuisance drunk. Nobody that I'd seen so far had been a violent drunk. Kazanzec arrived in his rubber dinghy with a young Buryat man he'd been fishing with, and who at first glance looked almost indistinguishable from a North American Indian. Kazanzec was a little unsteady on his feet too, but was as warm and attentive as ever, giving me a tender kiss on the cheek when he left. Then I cried.

I realised I was beginning to 'rest in natural peace' as the Buddhists say, like a slab of butter in the sun, losing its hard edges and becoming soft in the middle. Kazanzec was just one of many Baikal people who had helped me move towards that centre, but now I had to let go of them too. The creation beliefs of the Buryat people encompass the concept of Mother Earth and Father Sky; Lake Baikal is the great eye of the Earth Mother keeping watch over her children. She had most certainly been watching over me, and the magic of this special place stayed with me as I prepared for the long train trip that would take me into Kazakstan. My goal was Mount Belukha in the remote north-east — the mountain known to the shamans as Shambhala, the place where heaven and earth meet.

To Mount Belukha

At Irkutsk railway station I sat for five hours waiting for my train. The baggage room had closed for the night and there were few people around, but I was unwilling to leave my pack and go for a walk. I'd already had my daypack surreptitiously unzipped as I stood in a packed bus in this city, and a small purse containing personal items stolen. I sat, read, wrote, prowled around the waiting room that filled and emptied like the ebb and flow of a tide as local trains came and went. At 1.00 am the train from Mongolia arrived, and panicking a little as a surge of tired passengers pushed onto the train, at last I found the carriage my ticket had been issued for, but my bed was occupied and the occupant, fast asleep. In another tiny compartment that smelt of fish I found an empty bunk, but I was smartly moved on by the attendant. She was barely more than a metre tall and almost as wide, with a huge topknot of dyed blonde hair. Slinging my heavy pack over her shoulder as if it were a handbag, she marched me through eight carriages before dumping my bag at the feet of an even shorter man, telling him I had to have a bed. He complained. *'Bilyet Afstralii'* I said indignantly, having had to buy this ticket out of Russia before I left Sydney, to comply with visa regulations. He gave me a bed in an empty compartment, brought sheets to me for my last ten roubles and gave me a sleazy little stroke across my breast as he left, leaving me with an instant dilemma. Should I fasten the door with a strap after locking it? The attendants have keys and can walk in at any time, but if I strap it shut and someone from a late-night station stop needs one of the beds, they won't be able to get in, and in my tired state I may not hear pounding on the door. Compromising, I looped the belt over so he couldn't ease himself quietly into the compartment, but could open the door enough to shout at me.

Lying down to sleep I suddenly heard, as clear as a bell, Mum's voice saying in a somewhat reproving tone 'Chris*tine*, don't be so silly,' so I got up again thinking how stupid, he's much shorter than me and would probably lose his job if he tried anything, so I took the belt off and went to sleep.

Buddhists believe death is simply an initiation into another form of life. Was my mother travelling with me, reminding me to practise freedom from fear? I couldn't afford to be reacting to fear or anger for that matter; my experience with the Chinese minibus touts had clearly shown me the consequences of a rigid, angry mindset, seeing only aggression and injustice. I realised there was an important distinction to be made between relating from a position of fear, when what we see threatens us, and relating to fear but not feeling frightened.

This train, unlike the Trans-Mongolian Express, was dirty inside and jolted too much for me to write or even read very much. I'd been joined in the morning by a family of three, a sad-mouthed mother with her son and daughter who communicated little with each other or with me, although we shared lunch — their hardboiled eggs, cold potatoes and tomatoes, and my dried fruit and nuts. It was steaming hot but the windows in the compartment wouldn't open, and nor would the one opposite in the corridor. I lay in a sweaty stupor for most of the day, getting up before dusk to film the numerous children in the carriage. They had already seen me trying to film the passing landscape through the grimy windows, so when the camera came out again they were ready, racing surreptitiously to place themselves in front of it, their faces expressionless, solemn. The Russian-crewed trains were indisputably ruled by the carriage attendants. The short man had disappeared during the night and been replaced by another stout blonde, a despot who was quick to remonstrate, loudly and vehemently, hands on hips and arms akimbo if someone dared to do the wrong thing. Who cared if they lost face? Perhaps that was why everyone was so quiet.

At Novosibirsk, the city that marks the western edge of Siberia, I had to change trains again. The open sleeping compartment was full, the heat still unrelenting and I lay on my bottom bunk with a wet towel draped over my face, trying to ignore the saccharine music blaring from the tinny speakers. The all-pervading smell of fish was missing — we were a long way from Lake Baikal now. A large Kazak woman with a complete set of gold front teeth, that could be glimpsed occasionally in her conversation, appeared to have designs on my bed for her son, a strange, withdrawn young man. Unable to produce a ticket, she waited until nightfall and after installing him on the recently vacated top bunk opposite me, proceeded to improvise a bed for herself on the tiny space of floor. It was impossible to move. We broke the ice when her son, with much prompting, asked me my name and my age in English. When I replied, 'fifty-one', Katya (the woman) was enormously pleased and gave me a thumbs-up and a great golden gleaming smile. Women were often impressed to hear how old I was, and that I was alone, and were always incredulous that I didn't have a husband.

Katya's blank-faced son puzzled me. As we waited together at the end of the corridor to use the filthy, cramped toilet, he silently thrust his face into mine, and brought his body up very close. I gently and firmly pushed him away with my rumpled roll of toilet paper. He simply nodded. And as I crouched over the swaying toilet bowl, trying to keep the unlockable door closed and struggling for balance, he aggressively pushed the door open, his face expressionless. The second time he did this I flung the door open and yelled in English, 'I'll flatten you if you try that again!' Katya was there immediately, murmuring and patting me reassuringly on the shoulder, and I suddenly comprehended the situation. The boy was clearly deeply disturbed, and I wondered whether it was as a result of radiation poisoning — after all, we were on our way to Semipalatinsk in Kazakstan, the town that sits on the steppe just 150 kilometres from the Russian military's former nuclear testing site. Over a period of forty years it is estimated that more than 500 nuclear devices were tested at the place referred to as the Polygon. Some of the devices were high above ground, some were at ground level and, since 1963 when an international moratorium brought atmospheric testing to a halt, the rest have gone underground. The tests were only halted in 1989, leaving a terrible legacy for the people of the region, a people who had been unwitting human guinea pigs for the Soviet scientists. With this understanding came calm and compassion for Katya. No wonder she babied her son.

Later in the morning, as we neared the Kazak border, the train stopped in the middle of nowhere. *'C'est commerce!'* said my new friend Natalia, a cardiologist from St Petersburg, who was travelling with her son Petre to Semipalatinsk to commemorate her mother's death, 25 years before. She spoke French and her son spoke English and we'd teamed up after meeting in the baggage line at Novosibirsk railway station. A man with a flag and an orange railway waistcoat stood impassively on a strip of concrete as a sudden burst of activity issued forth from train windows — at breakneck speed, dozens of cartons were hurled out, some splitting open onto the tracks, and a huge mound of goods accumulated in the dusty grass: cooking oil, socks, toilet rolls — the paraphernalia of everyday life. Passengers hung out of other windows and good-naturedly cheered the 'traders' on, but the engineer was getting impatient, blowing the train whistle with mounting frustration as the last of the boxes were unceremoniously thrown onto the pile. I wanted desperately to film this hilarious cross-border 'smuggling' trade, but not at the risk of having my camera broken by someone who might wish to remain anonymous.

We chugged off again, close to Semipalatinsk now, and at a tiny station near the border the moneychangers arrived. Smiling young women with large bulging purses stuffed full of roubles and tengge made speedy progress through the train. When Natalia told me what exchange rate they were calling, I chased one of these fast-moving women down in the next carriage and — heart-in-mouth, perched on someone else's bunk — struck a deal. It was the culmination of a very odd trip; our arrival in Semipalatinsk felt almost like an anticlimax.

With all the planning in the world, I have never managed to make a journey that has been linear and predictable, and this one was no exception. There was no one to meet me at the station, but the woman selling papers outside helped me buy a token for the public phone. After some anxious searching I located the phone number for Victor and Lena, given to me by an Australian travel agent. I had made arrangements for this part of the trip before I left Sydney, knowing it would be difficult to travel this last leg to Mount Belukha on my own. Belukha is the highest peak in the remote Altai mountain range that straddles the meeting point of Russia, Mongolia, China and Kazakstan. The shamanic culture of Siberia and Central Asia is said to have evolved in a prehistoric heartland in these mountains, a culture that goes back to the ice age. Mount Belukha is revered by the Siberian shamans as a sacred dwelling place of gods and the site of Shambhala. I had been determined to reach this place since I first read of its existence.

Victor arrived at the station half an hour late, delayed by a flat battery. The agent had arranged for me to travel to the mountain with a group of climbers who were to pick me up the following day from his house, but Victor told me they had left two days before I arrived. As this was one of the few formal arrangements I had made, I was baffled. After a breakfast of eggs and bread and, later, a *banya* at Victor's mother's house (there was no hot water in the entire town, unless you produced your own), my friendly host rang the travel agent's contact in Semipalatinsk. The contact was apologetic, but insisted there was no public transport to Mount Belukha. He could, however, arrange a private taxi for me, for just US$200. Would I be interested? I declined — I didn't have that sort of spare cash.

Disconsolate and close to tears, I sat on a squeaky iron bed in my little room, weighing up the options. I'd had my heart set on this part of the journey. It had become its central core, resonant with myth and mystery, and I very much wanted to be at the mountain. The grief I felt over my mother's sudden death was still sharp and painful and I was even more strongly drawn to the notion that this place — Mount Belukha — might offer some sort of solace. Victor and Lena knew about the concept of Shambhala. Victor taught comparative religion, and they were both practising Baha'is. I had Baha'i friends in Australia but this homestay had been arranged through the anonymity of the Australian travel agent, and it was only when I recognised a picture of the Baha'i Lotus temple in New Delhi hanging on a wall in the living room that the penny dropped. Since spending time at art school with a Baha'i woman (we'd taken a dance unit together) I'd been very attracted to the philosophy. The belief that humanity is a single people with a common destiny directs their work in breaking down prejudice between people. As the founder, Baha'u'llah said, 'The Earth is but one country, and mankind its citizens.'

I now had some serious thinking to do. My fellow citizens the climbers had forced a change of plan, but I had no idea what to do next. I felt lost; Mount Belukha could have been a million kilometres away. Like most people I tended to assume that security lies in things being unchanging — an arrangement made gives a feeling of security in a strange place, just as a person who has always been in our life, who lives in a place we know intimately, gives us a sense of security. Then, that arrangement disintegrates, that person dies, that place you know so well is sold and the seemingly permanent connections to childhood are lost. When I went back to my growing-up place a year after this journey, the place had been transformed into a bed and breakfast establishment. I stood on the bank overlooking the beach at the front of the house and wept with anguish. Letting go of that place continues to this day. Intellectually I understand that impermanence is the only constant in our lives, but letting go and surrendering to the dance of transience is another matter altogether. Right now I felt the ground under me had shifted — a prompt to stop grasping at the idea of getting to the mountain. Despondent but almost resigned, I started to think about catching the next train out of town.

I spent the afternoon at the Dostoevsky Museum (the great Russian writer spent five years of exile in Semipalatinsk), arriving back in the evening with a postcard of his writing desk; a badly lit photograph of the table I had lovingly run my hands over when the attendant wasn't looking. My father had been passionate about Dostoevsky and particularly passionate about the translations of Constance Garnett. Old books of her translations, obviously considered too decrepit for the reading public, were held in the library where I worked, so I'd smuggled a few of them out from the basement stacks to the amusement and gratitude of my father. Surprisingly, I had also met an Australian in town, a brash but likeable young man who managed a mine outside Semipalatinsk for a Western Australian company. We met as I trailed up a bakingly hot footpath in search of the museum. He was so surprised to see a tourist with guidebook in hand that he crossed the road to speak to me. Tourists were obviously a rarity here.

Back at the flat I watched some of Victor's favourite videos with him. He was a great fan of B-grade Hollywood action movies, which dubbed in Russian were almost surreal. After dinner we spoke about the virtues of the Baha'i faith and about Shambhala, an odd counterpoint to the violence I'd just witnessed on the small screen. In talking to these people, I was reminded of the need to let go of my strong desires for what was 'supposed' to be, and start trusting that what happened was okay. I needed only to reflect on the chain of events that led me to the houseboat on Lake Baikal to realise that surrender in this sense was a more active principle than desire. But I also could not complacently sit back and trust that something good would happen. Still uncertain what to do and feeling more upset than I was showing, I retreated to my bedroom and asked the 'powers that be' (my father's phrase) for a sign.

The answer I needed came very quickly. Lena had urged me to stay on several times, and that evening she said quite casually, 'You know you can get a bus up the Bukhtarma Valley to Katon Karagay, why don't you stay?' I was ecstatic — there *were* two ways to get there, and I could do this route on my own! The guidebook listed a *gastinitsa* (hotel) at Katon, and buses going on to a village called Berel that sat at the base of the mountain. It would be a long, slow journey and necessitate getting to the next big town, Ust Kaminogorsk, to pick up the bus, but Lena arranged for two friends, also Baha'is, to meet me there.

Her friends were a young couple, very much in love. I had not yet registered with OVIR, the Passport and Visa Department of the Interior Ministry, because Victor forgot, so Olga and Slava gracefully took charge. First we went to the bank to fill out the form for registration and pay a small fee, then, with the temperature already in the mid-thirties, we walked across the river and down to the building at the given address. No they say, it's the old kindergarten building down the road, so we trudged off again only to find this building had a different sign on it — nothing to do with foreigner registration. We were then told to go to the Sputnik Building. We had to take a train, but by the time we arrived the building had just closed. Perhaps one of the big hotels would register me? First we went to the Ust Kaminogorsk Hotel with its street cafe draped in jungle-green netting, but they wouldn't register me either. Hungry, we retreated to the airconditioning of Olga and Slava's favourite pizza cafe where I was horrified to see my big, scarlet, sweating face reflected in the mirrors around the cafe. Even petite Olga with her enormous eyes was wilting a little, eyelids drooping with the heat and exhaustion of the foreigner registration process. The next hotel wouldn't register me either, or give me a room, although the place seemed very empty. Perhaps they didn't like the look of my face. We gave up.

The bus from Ust Kaminogorsk to Katon Karagay was ancient, very small, and there was no place for storing luggage. It was also overcrowded. I had been given a seat opposite a young boy and an old man, who had piled all their luggage into the space where my feet should go. Next to me a young woman balanced a large bassinette on her knees, her mother standing in the aisle to help her. It seemed they wanted me to take the mother's seat in the back row of the bus, so I gallantly squeezed in beside a man — the father? — who smelled strongly of alcohol, but there was just enough room to extend my right leg, as my hip was still very sore. No one wanted a window open, and the petrol fumes issuing from behind the back seat were visible to the naked eye. No wonder everyone fell asleep! Except of course the foreigner, unaccustomed to the spine-jarring bumps, and determined to see as much of the countryside as possible through the dirty little windows. It was impossible for me to film.

Hours later as we wound up into higher country, leaving behind the dry dustiness of the steppes, we passed through great fields of sunflowers in full bloom, spread out across wide valleys between two ranges of hills or tucked into the corners of hay or barley fields, and sometimes just

a sweeping golden glow between two ranges of distant mountains. A riot of wildflowers of every conceivable colour, shape and size lined the roadsides. Luminous wild white hollyhocks danced in village gardens and swayed on hillsides in a light breeze as we ground on into the afternoon. Horses wearing a semicircular harness over their necks pulled carts spilling over with fresh-cut grass, their drivers, handsome Kazak men. We passed cemeteries with open, pagoda-like structures over the graves that reminded me of tiny mosques, and on the hillsides marmots kept a watchful eye on the eagles circling quietly overhead.

No one spoke English on the bus, but in my stumbling Russian I managed to ascertain that there was no hotel at Katon Karagay, not even a guesthouse. The nearest place to stay was at Rakhmanovskie Klyuchi, 130 kilometres further on from the town, and we would be arriving in Katon late that evening. But I hadn't counted on the extraordinary bush telegraph that was transmitting as soon as the bus made its first stop in the small, darkening Kazak township. As I struggled with my big pack through the narrow door of the bus, at the stop I was told was mine (with a casual fling of the arm), the first people were already there, waiting for me.

The first two men, who had driven up in a small Russian jeep, offered to take me to Rakhmanovskie Klyuchi for US$200. I laughed, wondering if it would be safe to sleep under a tree. I couldn't blame them for assuming that all Western tourists were wealthy — in their terms, we were, but their price was my budget for two weeks! Other offers followed and everyone waited. Finally, a woman with two small boys walked over and I asked her what the fare should be — '3000T (US$35) return fare,' I repeated to the men with jeeps, who walked away in contempt. I was ready to give up, find a tree to sleep under, and catch the bus back next day. The renewed hope I had been feeling was fading fast.

And then Alexey appeared. A slim man of Russian heritage, he had an open face and a wide smile, and he agreed to take me to the Klyuchi — for 3000T. The men in jeeps drove off, and Alexey loaded my pack into his small car, a Lada. Putting my trust in strange men was beginning to be a habit, but my options were looking decidedly slim as evening neared. His house was on the outskirts of town. It was an unpainted timber house like most houses in the town, set inside a high wooden fence. A large vegetable garden ran down the side of the house and a narrow path around the perimeter led to the outhouse at the bottom of the garden. A muddy track ran in front and a fast-flowing stream hissed past the bedroom window. A beautiful late evening light hung over the damp hills and from the valley came the sound of animals coming home for the night. Further down the street a man shod his horse in the fading light. Alexey lived here with his wife Anna, his aunt and his grandmother, a shadowy woman who rarely ventured forth from her room. Anna was tall, dark and slender, with a kind face. She immediately busied herself in the kitchen making piles of fried eggs with bread and tea, and soon we were 'discussing' my trip to Mount Belukha, in phrasebook Russian. It seemed there was a problem I hadn't foreseen. Mount Belukha sits on the border with Russia, and a special permit is needed to go there — I could go to Rakhmanovskie Klyuchi, and no further. The permit took four working days to arrange and could only be obtained in Ust Kaminogorsk, the town I had just come from, a day's travel on the bus. It would mean an extra week that I couldn't afford on my visa.

So Rakhmanovskie Klyuchi was to be my destination. I could go for walks in the woods and to the waterfalls, and I felt I could be content in this wilderness, close to the fabled mountain, even if I couldn't set foot on it. Friends of Alexey's had arrived during dinner and it was now time for the men to look intently into the Lada's engine compartment, and for the phone to start ringing. I had no idea what plans were afoot, but I was constantly reassured that everything would be alright in the morning — I would be leaving for the Klyuchi at 6.00 am. Although I had reservations about Alexey's small car making it over the high mountain roads, I trusted these people implicitly and, feeling an enormous sense of relief, lay down to sleep on the couch Anna had made up for me.

The shrill sound of the alarm clock woke me at 4.45 am. I feigned sleep, longing to be horizontal for a few minutes more but Anna got up to make breakfast, and then Alexey appeared, dressed in full army uniform. He was a soldier! Breakfast was served with a solid tumbler of sweet red wine ('Drink! Drink!') and wild strawberry jam to spread on thick slices of homemade bread. At 6.00 am our transport arrived — an army jeep complete with a two-star Kazak soldier who moved over to let Alexey drive, then collapsed into sleep against the juddering door as soon as we drove off. Perched on the high back seat of the jeep, a grin from ear to ear, I waved goodbye to the generous Anna, feeling quite regal and special. It was wonderful to be on the move, and so close now to the mountain. At the edge of a small village not far out of town we drew up in front of a gate that closed the road, attended by a tired soldier. Jerking upright into a smartish salute when he saw who was in the jeep, he flung the gate wide open and waved us through. As I turned in surprise to look back, I suddenly realised how lucky I'd been. This was the post where passport details and intentions were taken down, and I had no registration. I was through without a second look.

We climbed steeply above the Berel River, the road so

rough and rutted the Kazak soldier was shaken out of his sleep. On a sharp bend the jeep stalled. With no room to turn the vehicle around the Kazak crash-started it in reverse. The jeep moved sedately down the slope towards the steep drop to the river. The engine fired just as my heart threatened to stop. I applauded. Mist still clung to the mountainsides as we drove slowly on, Alexey back at the wheel and the two men now peering intently into the forest, searching for something — a tree, a particular sort of pine tree, but I didn't fully understand. We stopped, and when Alexey bit hard into a green pinecone, thrown down to him by the Kazak soldier who was now swaying in the top branches of a tall pine, it dawned on me. In Sardinia a few years earlier I'd learned to identify the trees that produced pinenuts for eating, laboriously cracking the hard outer layer open to retrieve the small kernels, but these ones were fat and juicy, the cones green and soft enough to rip into with our teeth, revealing the long, soft white fruit lying hidden in the inner layers. A tiny, rich morsel of food. Later I learned to soak the cones in hot water, the peeling then made even easier — a great way to kill time on a long train journey.

Rakhmanovskie Klyuchi is a sanatorium situated in a remote forested valley in the shadow of Mount Belukha, where radon gas in the local mineral spring water is used by Kazak doctors to heal a variety of ailments. Passing through a small Kazak village whose entire population worked at the Klyuchi, we arrived at the cluster of buildings spread out across the narrow green valley. A big group of men and women from Ust Kaminogorsk was staying in the dormitories, and there Alexey introduced me to Varya, the only person who spoke English. She was an easy-going, tall, blue-eyed blonde, and a translator for the big nuclear components factory in Ust. Varya took charge, settling me into a dorm with five other women who worked in the same factory. They made me tea from wild blackcurrants and small black leaves from the forest, called *badan*, and I felt very welcome. Alexey departed, promising to come back for me in three days. In the dining room — a dingy, sparsely furnished room where basic meals of broths and dumplings and bread were eaten with aluminium cutlery that made my fillings ache — I was introduced to the rest of the group, and seated beside a *babushka* (a grandmother) and her eleven-year-old grandson.

The physician in charge of the Klyuchi was young, blonde and attractive. Doctor Marina had been here only three months herself but said she loved the isolation and the landscape in particular. She took my blood pressure, pronouncing me very fit to take the baths, and told me I looked great for my age. She also said I could 'bravely travel on' and I thanked her, wondering if she was being ironic or simply kind and poetic. Knowing something of the history of radiation poisoning in the region to the west, I was a little wary of immersing myself in radon-saturated water, but the people from Ust had been coming here for years and looked vibrantly healthy. Marina explained that 'Yes, radon 222, an inert gas, is indeed a radioactive substance but it is necessary for the life of each living organism — each cell. Obviously this is not a high level of radiation, which would be harmful to the organism' … that is, to my body. I wanted to believe her.

The Klyuchi was named after a hunter called Rakhmanov who lived at the beginning of the twentieth century in a small village about 50 kilometres away. One day in the *taiga* he shot and wounded a maral, the native deer that lives in these forests. It ran off, but he followed it to a lake into which it had plunged. Although seriously wounded, the maral had emerged from the lake completely healed. So surprised was the hunter that he swam in the lake too, and found that all the cuts and abrasions he had incurred in the chase were also healed. He returned to his village and told the people about the lake and its properties, and thereafter, people came here to be healed. Marina was adamant that immersion in the water was beneficial for skin ailments, gynaecological problems and bones, but we were to keep the heart-to-head area out of the water. I was naturally dubious, but on the other hand I didn't want to be seen as the foreign eccentric, and I wanted to get to know these people as much as I could in the short time I had here. And perhaps it would help my hip? I took the plunge.

The women bathed in the afternoon, the men in the morning. The water was quite hot and crystal clear, and at the bottom of the pool lay the 'Motherstone'. It's said that if you sit on this stone you will conceive very quickly. I stayed right away from it. There was a refreshing lack of false modesty among the women, who looked at one another's bodies quite openly and were playful in a non-judgemental, non-sexual manner. I was beginning to suspect that it might be more than the waters that healed wounds in this place.

Most of the women wanted to know if I was afraid to be travelling alone. I said, 'What is there to fear?' but I understood these women probably couldn't do what I was doing, the 'rules' were different. There's a certain privilege about being a foreign, single, older woman traveller in an untouristed area where you're not a part of any social system — including a 'tourist trail'. What I did have to do was to keep my antennae waving, to be intuitively alert for signs that all was not well. But here, all was particularly well. Varya insisted on carrying my camera bag and tripod everywhere I filmed; she translated interviews, took me for the walks I had anticipated and showed me where to find the black *badan* leaves we brewed for tea. I was looked after as if I was someone very special and it sometimes perplexed me. I hadn't yet told her about my mother so she wasn't simply feeling sorry for me, nor had I mentioned very much about the nature of the film, but she was completely unselfconscious in her acts of kindness, and others behaved similarly. Four days ago they didn't even know of my existence, yet their loving welcome and total acceptance was immediate and generous. I was a little resistant for a while, tried to carry my own gear, saying 'No, no, I'm fine' when a hand was extended to help me up a slope, until Varya remonstrated with me. 'Christine, please accept that we want to care for you.' So I did, and it felt very good.

Each day after the bath we explored the surrounding countryside. The lake has no fish and no vegetation, as the quantity of radon gas in the water prohibits the development of any natural ecosystem, but the *taiga* provided abundantly — wild strawberries and blackcurrants, salad greens, juicy pinenuts and wild mushrooms that we picked and hung to dry across the windows of the dormitory. Varya also introduced me to the small bar that thudded every night with Russian hip-hop music and Boney M songs. I shared a table with the 'five pretty women', a title selected by the men of course, and Masha and Varya. Varya was not a pretty woman in the conventional sense, but she had a strong face and her confident gaze was attractive in itself. Masha was a little older, petite, with a slightly startled look and enormous glasses, and then there was me, with a short haircut usually reserved for the men in this country, weatherbeaten and already a little bowed in the shoulders from carrying my enormous pack — and with no party clothes. I wanted to drink beer, but they insisted I drink the local fortified fruit wine, a strong sweet brew that foretold a nasty hangover. I was circulated around the tables. Marie, a lawyer from Ust, took me over to her table where one of her friends, already quite drunk, wanted to speak the only words of English she knew. 'I love you, I love you, I love you,' she said, rocking with laughter, gold teeth gleaming each time the coloured lights over the bar winked on. I danced a jerky quickstep with a very intense man whose name I forgot; twirled around the floor with a tall Kazak man, his girlfriend beaming on the sidelines; and rocked on to old Boney M songs with the barmaid who was easily the best dancer in the room and utterly uninhibited. She was a well-built woman, plain, dressed in her work clothes, but unlike the clubbers in the Mongolian nightclub her movements were confident, earthy and sexy. She soon had an appreciative circle around her, clapping and cheering her on. The dancing continued well into the night.

One clear day we walked to the top of the ridge to view Mount Belukha in her twin-peaked glory. Locals told me it wasn't often she revealed herself — cloud often obscured the high peaks. We trudged through meadows

Gobi Desert, Mongolia: on top
of Chongoryn Els, the singing sands.

Gobi Desert, Mongolia:
Erdenebeligi's 'ger' at Yolyn Am.

Gobi Desert, Mongolia:
sketching our host in his 'ger'.

Terelj, Mongolia: the huge rocks on the ridge resembled a woman with hands clasped in prayer.

Lake Baikal, Siberia: the houseboat became my refuge.

Olkhon Island, Lake Baikal, Siberia: sacred Buryat shrine.

Mt. Belukha on the Kazak-Russian border, the shamanic Shambhala.

Uzbekistan: Bukhara's bazaars are full of beautiful colours and shapes.

Samarkand, Uzbekistan: Shohi Zinda or 'the street of tombs' is a holy place.

Shakhrisabz, Uzbekistan: the remains of Timur's fourteenth-century summer palace.

Kokomeren Canyon, Kyrgyzstan:
one of the most rugged places
in Central Asia.

Xinjiang Province, western China:
Lake Karakul and the Pamir Mountain

abundant in wildflowers, mosquitoes and biting ants. The mosquitoes were huge, vociferous, and seemed to hunt in large packs. Turning to look back across the lake I could see the mountains that bordered China, just 40 kilometres away. The top meadow was covered in large, violet-blue flowers called *vodosbor*. I picked my way through them — it seemed criminal to crush them — so I was totally unprepared for the breathtaking sight that confronted me as I rounded the last crest. Suddenly, unexpectedly, Belukha rose up in front of me. The mountain had great presence even as part of a range of very interesting mountains. It had a north and a south peak separated by a snow-filled scooped basin with two obvious glaciers at the bottom. Dominating the skyline, Mount Belukha's imposing shape reminded me of a huge spaceship about to take off into unknown realms. Clouds were piled up behind it, enhancing the majesty of the scene. The steeply falling meadow in front of me was thick with *vodosbor* and the Berel River below was bordered by the dark-green taiga. A horse track on the opposite bank of the river was visible. Had I arrived with the climbers and my special permit, I would have been on that track, on my way up the mountain.

The Chinese believe it's acceptable to climb sacred mountains, like the five sacred peaks of Wu Tai Shan, but in the Hindu and Tibetan traditions this is not encouraged. The reason lies in the symbol of the mountain as ascension towards the Absolute, towards transcendence of the human condition. We are always on our way up the mountain, whether we're crossing the first stream in the foothills or struggling towards the summit, but to stand on the summit is almost a profanity because it signals the end of the urge to climb any further and negates the difference between God, the summit, and humankind — the climber. Perhaps I was more firmly on my own path because I had been left behind?

In that field of violet-blue I gazed at the mountain I had travelled so far to see, my mind and heart busy in a dialogue of conflicting emotions. As I sat there, I knew that what I was looking for was not in this particular place — Mount Belukha was beautiful but it was just a mountain. A sacred mountain to be sure, but I suddenly realised the Shambhala that I was searching for lies in a number of qualities found in any number of people — strangers who were constantly stepping forward to help me, to care for me and offer love and support. Shambhala was a state of mind. As the great Buddhist teacher Chogyam Trungpa says:

> The kingdom of Shambhala ... is the realm of the cosmic mirror, the primordial realm that is always available to human beings if they relax and expand their minds.[7]

In learning to trust, in starting to free myself from accepting and rejecting, I was witnessing the basic goodness that exists in all human beings. Varya and her friends, ordinary people with good hearts, were actively nourishing and practising kindness, healing my sore heart in ways I could not have imagined. We were all standing on the sacred mountain and all we had to do was keep ascending.

Belukha was the goal where I sought to find some unknown treasure, the pot of gold at the end of the rainbow, but if it was just a place-symbol for a state of being, then the recognition that the real treasure lay in my heart — in everyone's heart — was my real arrival at the mountain. The very act of going there had triggered a new awareness for me of my place in the world and a sense that the inner me was somehow being restored to health. Although no modern-day shaman had taken astral flight to heal me (at least none that I knew), I began to think about the similarities between the path I was on and the shamanic journey of initiation that had evolved in these mountains aeons ago: the presentation of some sort of ordeal, the journey, and the spiritual rebirth. It wasn't important that I hadn't experienced a revelation — I felt strongly the archetypal nature of such a journey. Although it was with reluctance I forced myself to move on with Varya's protestations ringing in my ears, it felt like the journey homeward was the beginning of a new path. It could be an equally circuitous route, but an opportunity to look at the same realities from different places and in a different context — I was in no hurry to leave Central Asia.

I was also in no hurry to leave the Klyuchi. I had just enough money to stay another few days, although it felt a little self-indulgent knowing how much ground there was still to cover. Varya had somehow found Alexey's phone number so we walked to the village, to the house with the telephone, only to discover the lines were dead. There had been no wind or rain for days, but Varya said it was because the villagers responsible for the telephone were drunk. At the Klyuchi the same morning I'd mentioned to Marie that I thought one of the attendants had multiple sclerosis, but apparently the weaving and jerking was also vodka-induced. With no way to contact Alexey, I walked back to the dormitory to pack, fragments of William Blake's poetry floating through my head:

He who binds to himself a joy
Does the winged life destroy;
But he who kisses the joy as it flies
Lives in Eternity's sun rise.[8]

Letting go is the path to real freedom in Buddhist teaching. My desire to stay on in this wonderful cocoon of affection could easily contract into an expectation that it would simply continue as long as I was there. Better to 'kiss the joy as it flies' and leave as we'd arranged.

Alexey and Anna had driven over in the Lada. Word spread that I was departing and the leave-taking suddenly became very emotional. I gave Varya a T-shirt she admired, and in return received a pair of thick socks she had knitted herself. Masha and Valla gave me pinecones they'd gathered and soaked for me, and then the group of women gathered on the verandah and sang Russian folksongs. Tears pricked my eyes as I sang my 'Summertime' song for them, and after many hugs and kisses we piled into the Lada. The small car coped easily with the mountain road. Whatever had been wrong with it a few days ago had evidently been fixed and, at the only engine-related halt, Anna and I happily gathered wild strawberries while Alexey checked out the motor. I thought Anna was excited to have me back. As we drove I frequently caught her gazing tenderly at me, obviously wanting to say something but lacking any words of English to express her thoughts. Without Varya to translate, we were somewhat frustratingly back to phrasebook Russian. At the top of the pass we stopped again. I turned to see Belukha rising in the distance behind us, the tops of both peaks encircled by cloud as if they had a secret to keep.

I shared a taxi back to Ust, an arrangement presumably made by Alexey and Anna some time during the night or very early the next morning. The arrangements they made always seemed mysterious. I had some understanding of spoken Russian, but in this household a mixture of Kazak and Russian was spoken and I was completely lost. We'd gone to bed well after midnight having taken a different route back to Katon, with a final stop at Alexey's mother's place for a *banya*, but at 8.00 the next morning a Kazak driver arrived at the house in his taxi. He would have arrived a lot earlier he said; but he'd had trouble with his *machina*. Fixing troublesome cars seemed to be a routine part of life here. I couldn't bear the thought of another tortuous nine hours on the bus back to Ust, but neither could I afford the luxury of a taxi on my own so I was enormously relieved to see three people who had been at the Klyuchi sitting in the car, waiting for me to farewell my hosts. It was another emotional moment; I'd come to love this couple. Clutching a bag of pinecones and a big jar of Katonsky honey I fumbled through words of goodbye as Anna cried openly. I promised to send postcards and a video of the film, certain I would never see my friends again.

Back in Ust Kaminogorsk I staggered onto my train for Almaty, completely and utterly exhausted, with a 24-hour rail journey ahead of me. It was a long, long way to the south of Kazakstan to Almaty and the Tian Shan mountains, and from there to Uzbekistan where I wanted to visit the fabled cities of the old Silk Road. The photographs from the Sydney cafe kitchen were still fresh in my mind, imbued in my consciousness, and although I'd found no traces of Shambhala in Uzbekistan, the lure of its ancient cities was irresistible. I couldn't leave Central Asia without seeing and somehow experiencing them.

Tian Shan means 'celestial mountains' and this range extends over 1500 kilometres from east to west, but is at its highest and most spectacular along its borders with China and south-east Kazakstan. Here there are hundreds of glaciers and dozens of summits over 5000 metres. I was still pursuing images which related to the theme of heaven and earth for my film. What could be more appropriate than this most heavenly of mountain ranges, which is revered by the indigenous peoples of the area and adored by serious trekkers and mountaineers? But by the time I arrived in Almaty, the old Kazak capital in the south-east corner of the country and the nearest large town to the high Tian Shan, unseasonably heavy rainfalls had turned the mountain trails into mud slides. Walking in the mountains would be impossible.

The Wide Open Sky

Almaty is a pleasant city, a cosmopolitan place by Central Asian standards and historically an oasis settlement on the Silk Road. I needed to obtain a visa for Uzbekistan here. I was glad to be forced to stop for a few days — to put the camera down, to give myself breathing space and take the load off my shoulders. My right hip and knee had been aching almost constantly since Mongolia. At times my leg was so sore I walked with a limp, but I'd had no chance to stop and rest, or even to keep up a regular yoga practice which I knew from experience would relieve the pain. I wasn't sleeping on the hard ground anymore, but nor had I encountered an innerspring mattress or even a soft one. The deep discomfort in my joints felt locked in place, unable to be released even in deep sleep. It wasn't simply the bad weather that would keep me off the mountain trails; in my present condition I doubted if I could walk uphill for more than a few minutes.

In Almaty I stayed with a young Kazak woman who knew Victor and Lena, the people I'd stayed with in Semipalatinsk in the north. Ziba was part Kazak, part Tajik and part Berber and, although she was much younger than me, we shared the same birthday. She was also a Baha'i. Tall and dark-haired with widely set features and a slightly gap-toothed, attractive smile, she was a self-contained young woman, not effusively welcoming, understandable since I had arrived at her flat at 4.30 in the morning, but warmly efficient and well organised. In some ways she reminded me of myself. I was sleeping in her bed, with my big pack and assorted camera gear filling her tiny bedroom but, because she was currently between jobs, the extra money I provided was very useful. She was a clothes designer in her spare time and dressed very elegantly, which most certainly was not like me.

The Baha'i connections had become uncanny. When I properly inspected the documents given to me by the Australian travel agent, I discovered that a man called Samad, working from a travel office in Almaty, was the original contact in Central Asia. It was Samad who arranged for me to stay with Victor and Lena, and now Ziba. It was Samad who organised the ill-fated climbing expedition to Mount Belukha, and now he had to deal with the problems generated by my failure to register when I entered the country. No one would care that I'd tried very hard to comply with the regulations. There would be a large fine, he thought. My heart sank — how on earth could I afford it, and what would I have to forgo to pay for it? He told me I would be required to have accommodation organised within Uzbekistan to get a visa — involving additional expenses — and warned me of the dangers of being there on my own. Realising his anxiety was genuine, I promised I would be especially careful with my documents, and email him as soon as I arrived in Tashkent.

After leaving his office I walked the four long, leafy blocks into the centre of the small city, stopping at an optometrist to have my reading glasses tightened. They'd been dropping off my nose at the most inopportune moments, usually when both hands were full. There was no technician in the shop but the manager offered to do the job himself, taking me into his back office and offering tea while I waited. Glad to sit and sip, I looked up to see the now familiar Baha'i calendar on the wall. Was half the population of Central Asia Baha'i? Apparently the owner of the shop also owned Ziba's flat, and this man, Omar, recently a refugee from Iran, had a flat in Bishkek, the capital of Kyrgyzstan where his wife, son and daughter lived. His children were at university in Bishkek but there was no work for him in Kyrgyzstan, so he spent long periods on his own here, supported by the Baha'i community, but lonely. His flat was in the centre of Bishkek, his children spoke English, and he insisted I stay with them when I went to Kyrgyzstan.

Omar gave me directions for the Uzbek Embassy and I set off to find the No. 16 trolleybus. At the bus stop, after waiting for some time, I made further enquiries of a young woman called Olga who politely reiterated, in excellent English, Omar's directions, then boarded her bus. Minutes later she was back. She'd disembarked at the next stop and walked back, anxious that I had the right information. We waited and waited. Finally Olga hailed a taxi, told me she was taking me herself to the embassy, and motioned for me to climb in. Minutes later we were at the front gates of the very plain house which housed the Uzbek consul, and as I tried to pay her the taxi fare before she drove off, Olga waved my proffered notes aside and said firmly, 'Take good fortune when it comes.' The powers that be were evidently not yet convinced that I had learned to let myself be looked after, but there would be other opportunities.

Ziba never rose early, for which I was immensely thankful. Remarkably, she had the latest Margaret Atwood novel in English, offering to lend it to me for my trip into

Uzbekistan. I was more than happy to sleep in, then stay in bed reading with a cup of tea next to me, trying not to be too avid as I dipped into the latest offering from this popular novelist, making sure I had something left to entertain me once I was on the road again. I had perused the bookshops of Almaty with little success. The English sections seemed to contain little else besides shelves of Charles Dickens and I had seen none of the miscellaneous collections of secondhand books usually found along backpacker trails. In fact, it was one such shelf of tattered secondhand books, at the back of a shop on a Greek island, that yielded the novel *Seven Who Fled*, the book which first sparked my passion to be in this place, to see the Tian Shan mountains and cross the deserts of Central Asia.[9] But then, this wasn't a backpacker trail — in fact I hadn't seen another backpacker since encountering two Germans in Irkutsk.

The next day I left Samad's office for the second time, overjoyed because he'd retrieved my passport from OVIR registration without incurring even a small fine. I walked into town to find a Georgian restaurant listed in the guidebook. I had a hunger for the hot cheese bread I'd first encountered some years before in Moscow. As I crossed the wide road a car, travelling quite fast, screeched to a halt beside me. A little alarmed I jumped onto the footpath but a figure hurled itself out of the front passenger seat and landed in front of me — it was the Australian I'd met on another footpath, a few weeks before in Semipalatinsk. Brett took me to a bar in the Soho Hotel, and there I met the expatriot crowd, the foreign business people of Almaty. Kazakstan is probably, in per capita terms, the richest mineral nation on earth, and now that the USSR had dissolved, the government was working hard to attract foreign investment into the enormous oil and gas reserves. Many of the men in the bar were fellow Australians involved in the business of minerals, but in my worn Indian shirt and faded trousers I felt like a foreigner among them. I didn't know what to talk about and I certainly couldn't keep up with the drinking, but Brett insisted I eat lunch on his tab, plying me with beer and coffee, and I accepted gratefully. It wasn't often I got to eat Western food. The bar could have been in Sydney's CBD, but I felt uncomfortable and awkward in my attempts to slip into the easy familiarity of Aussie smalltalk. In the past three months, nothing — not one event, meeting or conversation — had seemed small or insignificant.

~

Ziba promised to store some of my gear until I came back through Almaty. I was determined to make the border crossings into and out of Uzbekistan as painless as possible. I'd heard stories of harassment of independent tourists by

Uzbek officials and police, and a heavy pack could only hinder a quick getaway! A Tajik man told me that Uzbekistan wanted to leave the CIS — the Commonwealth of Independent States founded in 1991 and now including all the former Soviet republics except the Baltic states. The aim of the CIS was to have a common economic zone and a unified defence and peacekeeping system, especially important given the vulnerability of some areas such as the border with Afghanistan, and the nuclear arsenal of Kazakstan's north. But Uzbekistan had tightened up its borders, even abolishing the train link from Tashkent to Moscow. Keep the antennae waving I told myself, but don't anticipate trouble.

I made a spontaneous decision to stop at the village of Zhabaghly, in the far south-west of Kazakstan not far from the Uzbek border, before crossing into Uzbekistan. Zhabaghly sits at the base of the Talassky Alatau Range in the western Tian Shan mountains, and here the Aqsu-Zhabaghly Nature Reserve has been established, 750 square kilometres of mountain meadows, juniper forests and high peaks. Perhaps I was developing an intolerance for city living, but the idea of spending a quiet week in beautiful mountain meadows before stepping into the uncertainties of travel in Uzbekistan was very attractive.

The woman sitting next to me on the bus, an oil engineering student and model from Turkmenistan, shook me awake at 4.00 am. We had struck up a conversation when I realised I wasn't going to get much sleep in our seat at the front of the bus, as she and the driver had been talking non-stop since we'd left Almaty, and the bus was so full I couldn't change seats. She modelled to pay for her education and she'd chosen oil engineering simply because there were jobs in that industry. She was very tall and slender, with long black hair and a strong face and I could see why she might make a big success out of both career paths, odd though this combination seemed. I was dropped off at a town called Tulkibas. Even at this hour a few men were hanging around the bus stop. The bus driver and the model, who spoke a little English, arranged for one of them to drive me to the village, but I'd expected to arrive there in daylight and had only the first names of two couples who might provide accommodation, and the name of a street. The 'taxi' driver seemed unperturbed as he hammered on the door of the first house in the street, but it took just one rude awakening to get the right address — it was a small village and everyone knew Zhenia, the former director of the park. He made up a bed for me and went back to sleep. In the morning he arranged for one of the local horsemen, Valodia, to take me into the park on a three-day horse trek, and introduced me to Vladimir, the park's chief scientist.

Valodia lived next door to Vladimir and spoke a little

English. Although he was not a scientist, he was well versed in the flora and fauna of the park. He was an accomplished horseman, big, tall and muscular, and dark. I discovered it was the Tatar heritage (Tatars were a Turkik people of Russia) that gave these men, here and in Russia, their distinctive good looks, and these particular good looks were enough to make me a little weak in the knees. I wondered if I'd be able to properly mount my horse. Perhaps I'd need a hand up. Vladimir the scientist was an exceptionally sweet-natured man, knowledgeable and passionate about everything that grew, walked, crawled or flew in the park. He told me there are 1600 species of plants here, including many that I had taken for granted as being English cottage garden flowers without questioning their origins. There were also Bronze- and Iron-Age petroglyphs in the high meadows, and wild animals in the mountains, including the Isabelene brown bear, rare birds of prey, and the snow leopard. I had splendid visions of filming from horseback while riding through fields of wildflowers and encountering bears along the way, although I couldn't stretch my imagination to include a snow leopard. I'd have to be extraordinarily lucky to see one of those elusive beasts.

The village had been a gulag from 1862 to 1864 and remained very small until about fifteen years ago when a chicken factory was set up on the outskirts. The *zapovednik* (nature reserve) was established in 1926, but as there are fewer than fifty park staff, including rangers, scientific and technical staff, most people work in the factory or are subsistence farmers. The farmers were cutting hay that morning — tough mountain grasses spilled off carts and trucks as the farmers carried their golden loads to the winter storehouses in the village, leaving stubbled fields that were painful to walk across. Pure white hollyhocks occasionally nodded among the stalky debris, and children too young to be cutting and carrying this harvest rode their donkeys across to the swimming hole in the river.

Our expedition got off to a slow start. The director, who was to sign my permit for entry into the park, was in Shymkent and his assistant was nowhere to be found, but at midday we were ready. We would be sleeping in one of the two park huts, and Valodia had packed our food and our sleeping bags into two bulging saddle bags that were slung over the back of his enormous stallion. Male horses in these parts are never gelded; they need to be tough to survive the winters in these mountains. He'd saddled a two-year-old colt for me — a lovely horse for a relatively inexperienced rider, but a serious competitor as far as Valodia's stallion was concerned, and I grew to appreciate his nimbleness on the steep mountain trails. After stopping to admire a beautiful waterfall in a gorge of high red rocks we took a steep rough trail up a narrow side valley, crossing a small river before the climb. The stallion seized the moment, nipping my horse on the rump, plunging ahead of us and offering a swift kick broadside as he passed. To my astonishment I stayed on the colt's back as he reared in protest, stumbled on the river stones and eventually bolted up the track after the stallion.

It wasn't long before we discovered bear prints in the mud — the bears were using the same mountain track as us, tearing at the apple trees and junipers that lined the path to get the fruit and berries. I hoped any encounter with these animals wasn't going to be too unexpected! From horseback I could smell the small patches of dianthus, the delicate frilled flower we called 'pinks' at home, before we even saw them. Soon the mountainsides were filled with a knee-deep riot of wildflowers — purple delphiniums, yellow violas, blue geraniums, white hollyhocks, poppies and allium, gentians and columbines, asters, St John's Wort, chamomile and fennel. But it's not only the flowers of the 'English country garden' that are native to these mountains — there are thirty-three kinds of wild tulip in Kazakstan, the apple has its origins here, and even the Rufus turtle dove is native to Kazakstan and Siberia. My mother would have loved this place. I was still composing long, descriptive letters to her in my mind, bringing myself up short as, astonished and upset, I realised I no longer had a mother to write to. I wanted to paint word pictures for her and I knew she would have been equally fascinated to know that many of the flowers she tended so lovingly in her Ruby Bay garden had their origins here, and that I was gloriously among it all.

Our hut was set on top of a steep valley, nestled into a hollow filled with wild, white hollyhocks, apple trees and juniper. The juniper is a very slow-growing tree, gaining only about one centimetre per year in this climate. Some of the large gnarled trees on these slopes must have been ancient. The horses were tethered and Valodia cooked lunch over a fire outside the hut, insistently refusing any offers of help from me. Was I really allowed to do nothing? The sun shone, the warm breeze set the hollyhocks nodding, there were no biting insects and the only dangerous wild animal I had glimpsed, a small, richly patterned snake, quietly slithered away into a dark part of the woodshed adjacent to the hut. My sole task was to stir jam into my tea, a Russian taste I'd been introduced to in Siberia and an ongoing legacy in these parts it seemed. I liked it. That night we slept side by side on a hard raised platform at the back of the hut. Cloudless night skies had me stargazing, the foreign northern sky blazing with constellations that included vaguely familiar astrological patterns.

The following afternoon we rode up a narrow valley to the Marble mountains, where the frozen trail of one of last winter's avalanches snaked down to the meadows.

Delicate bright yellow poppies lined a small stream that was fed from the ice of the avalanche, and to the side of the trail we found the huge curved horns of an ibex, the native mountain goat. Vladimir told me later that the beasts are sometimes caught by the winter avalanches and hurled to their death down the mountain, to be discovered only in the summer melt. Valodia looked for ibex and bear on the top slopes — in summer the bears come down off the tops to feast on fruit and berries, retreating in winter to the snow for hibernation — but all we saw was a small, lone roe deer. Undeterred by the lack of visible wildlife Valodia led me up a steep ridge as dusk was falling, coaxing me higher and higher. 'Little bit on? Little bit higher?' As we rested near the top, panting from the exertion, we heard a roar! Peering cautiously over the lip of the ridge we saw two brown bears come ambling out of the junipers and down towards the stream below us. I prayed for them to come in our direction, hands fumbling for the camera, trying to find enough light and calm my breath. I had no tripod! The bears were playful, teenagers really, wearing the white band around the neck which signified last year's cubs. They stayed and played in the stream, tumbling and pushing each other off a ledge of ice, and we lay on the hill above them and chortled and sighed with delight.

Next day we rode to the top hut at 2000 metres, through meadows at times waist-high in wildflowers with invisible red marmots whistling their warnings and a blue whistling thrush giving us a higher tune. I wanted to see the Bronze-Age petroglyphs, pictures that had been carved into the sunlit surfaces of rocks on the edge of a steep valley. The carvings were mostly of ibex, which must have been plentiful here then, perhaps a major food source. It was exciting to imagine that three to four thousand years ago people had been sitting here admiring the same view and making these carvings, perhaps perceiving them as symbols imbued with a magical quality, an attribute that would establish a sacred relationship between the hunter and the hunted. It was an expansive vision, and I was reminded of another point that Chogyam Trungpa makes in his book on Shambhala.

> When human beings have no sense of living with a wide open sky above and a lush green earth below, then it becomes very difficult for them to expand their vision. When we feel that heaven is an iron lid and that the earth is a parched desert, then we want to hide away rather than extending ourselves to help others. Shambhala vision does not advocate going 'back to nature'. But within the world that we live in, there is room to relax and appreciate ourselves and our heaven and our earth … If we open our eyes, if we open our minds, if

> we open our hearts, we will find that this world is a magical place.[10]

It wasn't too difficult to feel the magic here, and to feel a stirring of unnameable satisfaction as the pressure of wanting certain things to happen simply faded away. Up here there was no need for complicated philosophies, but there was plenty of room for expansion.

Back at Zhabaghly village I stayed with Vladimir, the chief scientist at the Nature Reserve. His tiny house faced the mountains he knew so well, and loved so passionately. Down in the long, narrow back garden was the shower cubicle, a cramped outhouse with a drum perched on top, filled with water that was first heated on the stove. A tube with shower head attached hung down from the drum, and a plastic curtain barely covered the front of the cubicle. It faced directly into Valodia's garden. There wasn't enough room in the cubicle to undress and dress, so I tried to make the process as seemly as possible while keeping an eye on the neighbour's yard, just a couple of metres away. I wasn't even sure whether I might want to be caught! It was blissful having a hot shower. Most of the big Central Asian towns I'd stayed in had cold water only, as town councils took advantage of the hot weather to make repairs to the disintegrating underground water pipes, and although I had been given many *banyas*, the action of pouring water over my body from a dipper couldn't quite match the feeling of a cascade of warm water from above.

Vladimir was both an ornithologist and a botanist, and in recent years had been touring the United Kingdom, speaking about the park and its biodiversity. The following day he was to travel across the border to Tashkent — the nearest international airport — to pick up a group of botanists from the UK and bring them back to Zhabaghly for a study tour of the park. He would drive me to the border, guide me across the border post and take me on a local bus to the airport, where he was to meet the tour group. Uzbekistan has the reputation of being the most difficult of the Central Asian republics for solo travellers both to enter and move about in, and he was aware of the potential for bureaucratic pettiness at the border post. I was utterly relieved — another perceived obstacle had been gently removed.

Of Melons and Medressas

I was soon back in the heat and noise of a big city. Tashkent is the capital of Uzbekistan, though not the major destination for most travellers in this country. Within this mostly flat, monotonous landscape of desert, steppe, salt marshes and the sad remains of the once pristine Aral Sea (originally the world's fourth-largest lake until the central planners of the former USSR deliberately drained it for cotton production) lies some of the most splendid, audacious architecture in the east, in towns that are former centres of the Silk Road. Many of these beautiful buildings were constructed in the fourteenth century when Timur, Jenghiz Khan's descendant, was busy establishing a new empire in Central Asia. He was a notoriously savage ruler with an estimated seventeen million deaths attributed to his conquests, but he left a legacy of dazzling mosques, mausoleums, minarets and medressas (Islamic seminaries) in the towns he established. Timur sent back the best artists and craftsmen from the countries he defeated, along with huge armies of slaves to do the manual work, and built his glittering capital at Samarkand, a city that became the economic, cultural and later, under his grandson Ulughbek, intellectual centre of Central Asia.

At the age of sixty-nine Timur prepared to mount a campaign against the still unconquered China, but on his way east he was struck down by a fever and, in the words of his followers, 'coughed like a strangled camel and foamed like a camel dragged backwards with the rein'. 'We know of no cure for death,' said his doctors, and so he was carried back to Samarkand and laid to rest in the Guri Amir mausoleum, a building still being worked on by slaves from India, China and Persia. It seems, however, that Timur could not rest. Priests of the temple reported hearing him move every night for a whole year even though friends had given large sums of money to the temple so that he would cease his howling. The priests advised that the son be asked to set free the prisoners taken by his father in other countries, especially the craftsmen in Samarkand. Timur's son did let them go, and as soon as they were free the ghost of Timur ceased to howl. Or so the story goes.

My first goal in Tashkent was to find some traditional Uzbek clothes. It was very hot, well over forty degrees Centigrade, and I reasoned that the loose-fitting pants and dresses would not only be modest in this Muslim country, but provide some respite from the harsh, unrelenting heat. I had a sudden yearning to head back to Zhabaghly to the softness of the mountain air, the slow pace of village life and the company of my new friends, but I restrained myself and turned instead to the bustling bazaars of Tashkent.

I went first to the bank to change a traveller's cheque, an experience that had me choking on hysterical laughter as I waited in line behind an American man who was also buying local currency. He was being asked to fill in the same form, over and over again, and was becoming very agitated and quite paranoid, saying 'She is making a fool of me and I don't like it!' The stack of duplicate papers was stamped and filed, and after mine had been processed I was interviewed by a man who wanted to know why I had Australian cheques and a New Zealand passport. Then off to another room to get my money, but alas one of my papers had the wrong stamp on it, so back to the first line for the right stamp. An hour later I had my money, minus a three per cent commission. I was starting to understand where the rumours of 'petty bureaucracy' were coming from. It was not a user-friendly place.

The rattling No. 8 tram took me to the Chorsu Bazaar in the old city — a sprawling maze of market stalls covering an enormous area. The clothing market was huge and uninspiring, with row upon row of dowdy acrylic items that I'd seen for sale in every Chinese town I had visited, but at last, at midday as the temperature rose to almost 50°C, I found what I wanted. The trousers were very wide and baggy at the top and from the waist to mid-thigh were generally of a plain, bright fabric. The legs of the trousers were of a different fabric (patterned and in a different colour) and over them went a voluminous dress of yet another colour, in another pattern. The women wore headscarves with different colours and patterns again. Why, I wondered, do we in the West place such emphasis on matching outfits? The riot of colour and design was glorious. I couldn't wait to join the throng.

I spent many hours in the local bazaars of Uzbekistan. After their initial astonishment the local people were very pleased to see me wearing traditional dress and I received many compliments from women and especially, older men. It also gave me a kind of special permission when it came to filming in these places. As soon as the camera and tripod came out, interested spectators and performers alike surrounded me, and finding 'subject matter' or enthusiastic camera assistants was never a problem. At times the challenge lay in declining their services and, if they were fast enough to find the zoom control, any hope of usable footage was gone! The women in the Chorsu Bazaar dressed me carefully, amid gales of laughter and flashing gold teeth, and plied me with cups of tea when I looked like wilting in the fierce heat. I showed them how to use the camera, to film my dress-ups and a spoken piece to camera: 'Here I am, red in the face from too much Tashkent heat, feeling rather like a one-woman circus …'

My accommodation in Uzbekistan had been arranged by a woman called Anya, who frowned a lot, and was quite the opposite of Samad, who beamed frequently. Anya met me at Tashkent's small airport where I had reluctantly parted company with Vladimir, having been steered expertly through the intricacies and anxieties of the Uzbek border post and onto a local bus where we stood jammed like sardines in the aisle, nearly missing our stop because we couldn't get my big pack through the back door fast enough. Anya arrived late in an airconditioned four-wheel-drive vehicle with her driver, a meticulous man who drove with painstaking care through the narrow streets. My first impression of Anya was of a woman who got things done, but as I was to discover later, if things weren't impinging on her sense of wellbeing, she wasn't interested in doing much at all. She dyed her hair blonde but looked strikingly like a Thai woman, although she may have been ethnically Tajik. She'd booked a hotel room in Tashkent for me, and organised rooms in guesthouses in Samarkand, Bukhara and Khiva, towns which held some of the most outstanding Islamic architecture in Central Asia. It was up to me to arrange to get to these places.

I caught a local bus to Samarkand, a journey of five hours. The driver refused to stop for anyone or anything, not food, not toilets and especially not for the tantalising mounds of melons piled up on roadsides, even though the elderly, grey-bearded man beside me begged and pleaded with him. I'd had the forethought to bring a bottle of mineral water with me, but wasn't aware, at least not until we were well under way, with the bus full, that I'd chosen a seat facing into the sun. The temperature climbed rapidly, my face reddened and I sweated uncomfortably and copiously, even with all the windows open. I longed to sleep the hours away but my companion and the man behind him, both excited to be host to a foreign woman dressed as an Uzbek, felt compelled to point out every conceivably interesting thing we passed — cottonfields, mountain (a small hill), river, village, donkey (hot, tired donkey). The elderly gentleman nudged me in the ribs if my eyes threatened to close. It was a landscape almost devoid of interesting features, and after the lushness of the mountains seemed terribly parched.

I had finally aligned myself with the backpacker and tourist trail. Two young women who leapt onto the bus just as it pulled out of the yard in Tashkent were New Zealanders, from Wellington. As we disembarked at the bus station in Samarkand I moved over to talk to them, fighting off a melee of aggressive taxidrivers, including one man who simply picked up my pack without asking and put it in the boot of his car, leaving me to indignantly wrestle it out again before he climbed in and drove off. It was a shock to be back in a world of aggressive transactions and deceitful enterprise after my sojourn in the mountains. Even Tashkent felt gentle compared with this mayhem, but Samarkand was unquestionably a tourist town and there was money to be made. Anya had told me what to pay for a taxi to the old town centre. It was about a third of the sums being demanded, so I stood my ground until a driver gave in, taking the three of us the brief distance to our respective lodgings.

The guesthouse was a short walk through dusty narrow streets to the Registan, the medieval commercial, academic and religious centre and the centrepiece of old Samarkand. In the late sunlight the domes, minarets and decorative mosaics of the medressas glowed; the brilliant colours of the Persian-styled ornament lighting up the immense, beautifully proportioned forms. I sat with the two young New Zealand women on the raised platform of a *choyhona*, the local version of a teahouse, opposite the Registan, sipping a cold beer and trying to avoid the attentions of brash young men who swaggered uninvited up to our table. I'd been warned not to stay out after dusk in this town, the large population of aimless youth being one of the reasons. There were tales of bag snatching, unpleasant drunkenness and harassment of women travellers, and it was easy to get lost in the maze of narrow streets in the old town even in daylight. I decided to go to bed early and explore the town at first light, hopefully before the tour groups (and by extension the hawkers) converged on the sites I planned to visit.

It was as though several worlds tried to exist here, side by side. Inside the old town, in the sun-baked back streets away from the splendours of the Timurid architecture, it seemed the twentieth century had barely impinged on the daily life of the people, but hard up against it sat the sprawling, Russian-style part of the city with its shopping malls, wide avenues and groaning public transport system. The Registan with its gloriously decorated medressas was a spectacular sight, but it was like a busy museum. It was impossible to be alone to simply sit and look or draw without being accosted by hawkers or touts, or the ubiquitous bold youths of the town. I felt more comfortable in the quiet, spirit-filled street of Shahi Zinda (the street of tombs); and later, in the peaceful Labi-hauz plaza of Bukhara with its seventeenth-century pool, ancient mulberry trees and wonderful cross-section of people. In these places I began to have some understanding of what life could have been like when these were the intellectual, religious and commercial centres of Central Asia.

Shahi Zinda in Samarkand was unlike any other monument I saw. Its architecture distinctly different from the 'museum' architecture of the Registan, the street of tombs is a holy place of pilgrimage, containing what is probably the grave of Qusam ibn-Abbas, a cousin of the Prophet Muhammad, who reputedly brought Islam to this area. Most of the other graves belong to Timur's family and close associates; small, largely unrestored buildings that are decorated with the most beautiful majolica tile-work I had seen in the town. At sunrise the place was virtually deserted except for an old man with a brush broom carefully sweeping the entrance to the holiest of shrines. I'd remembered to cover my arms and wear a headscarf and so felt comfortable entering the square, domed chambers with their portal arches and narrow doorways. It was peaceful and cool. The sun's first rays were lighting the incomparable mosaics of blues that ranged from turquoise to the deepest sapphire, contrasting so exquisitely with the rich earthen golds and browns of the walls. Early morning was definitely the best time to be here. At the top of the cobbled path I stood on a low wall to look out across the city. The countryside surrounding it was already shimmering with heat and the sounds of the bazaar below, which was just starting to buzz with the day's business, drifted up the hill.

The gatekeeper, who doubled as dispenser of blessings, had just been given an offering of freshly baked bread as I came down the steps to leave. Having said the appropriate prayer over the woman, whose offering was now being eaten by the gatekeeper's friends, he motioned for me to sit and drink tea and share the still-warm bread as the woman plodded up the steep steps towards the city of the dead, seemingly unconcerned about the destination of her offering. My mother hadn't wanted to be buried — she'd asked for cremation, her ashes to be thrown into the bay where she loved to swim, in front of the house. I thought it was an act symbolic of freedom, letting go the last vestiges of the earthly body and it didn't much matter if you thought there might be another existence to follow, or not. It was the letting go that seemed important.

~

In Shakhrisabz, a small town about 100 kilometres south of Samarkand, I discovered the best melon markets. Timur was born near here in 1336. Kesh, as it was called then, was already an ancient town and the seat of Timur's clan. The town lies in a small valley surrounded by the foothills of the Pamir mountains and was renamed Shakhrisabz (Green Town) by Timur, who instructed his descendants to continue developing the town long after his death. His grandson Ulughbek complied, completing a big mosque and a family mausoleum in the mid-fifteenth century — both are still standing. I'd travelled there from Samarkand to see Timur's summer palace called Ak Saray, the White Palace. It must have been an extraordinary building, although all that's left now are the remains of the massive portal, a magnificent 40 metres in height, covered with beautiful, delicately patterned white and gold mosaics. It was an ambitious project even for Timur, taking twenty years to complete, but it was destroyed in the sixteenth century by the Emir of Bukhara, who is said to have been distressed by the stupidity of his act. Scanning the town from the top of the tower I could see the domes of ancient mosques and mausoleums dotted through the unremarkable back streets of the town, and a stream of people heading towards the markets. I clambered down the narrow circular stairway, the stone steps shaped by over 600 years of footsteps, and crossed the park, skirting wedding parties and their attendant cameramen who shouldered enormous old video recorders, past the large fountain where naked boys were dive-bombing into the shallow water, and joined the crowd.

The bazaar complex was built in the fifteenth century, and probably little had changed since then. Most of the food market was under cover though that didn't deter the swarms of flies that converged on the hunks of meat hanging from large hooks in the tiled recesses at the back of the building, disturbed only as the butcher carved off selected chunks for his customers. Huge white mounds of ricotta cheese covered the tables in the centre of the market, while the women selling eggs from coloured plastic buckets squatted in the shade thrown by the low wall at the front. The melons — hundreds of them — were piled in the courtyard below. Watermelons, large round yellow melons and long pale greenish-white ones called *dynya*, were stacked in pyramids around the yard, with their owners tucked in beside them under makeshift covers to keep off the searing sun. Potential buyers tapped the melons, sniffing them intently, presumably alert to the smell of ripened fruit under the thick skins. The merchandise moved fast and the melon sellers replenished their diminishing stocks from loaded carts on the edges of the courtyard. The fruit was thrown dextrously across to the stallholders by enthusiastic young boys, every one of whom wanted to get within camera shot. I was invited to sit inside the sea of watermelons, their smooth full shapes like great green buttocks glowing in the shade of the awning, to eat the dripping pink flesh and drink tea while my new camera assistant, a thin, dark young man wearing a Russian blue and white striped singlet and a smile from ear to ear, filmed all of his friends.

The small craft bazaars in the old parts of the cities were also a source of fascination and enjoyment. There is now a strong movement to revive the traditional crafts of the region that, in the days of Silk Road trading, were famous far beyond the Muslim East. These skills had been sadly neglected by the end of the twentieth century. In Samarkand I'd met musicians and makers of traditional stringed instruments, filming their craft and even singing a few wordless bars with a young musician who was very surprised to hear I had some idea of the phrasing of their music.

In Bukhara I planned to go shopping. Bukhara lies to the west of Samarkand, another five-hour bus ride away. I'd packed food for the trip this time — boiled eggs and bread — and tried not to drink too much water before we left, anticipating there would be no toilet stops. Sure enough the driver planted his foot on the accelerator and didn't take it off for the full five hours, slowing only to turn around in his seat and shout at people, evidently recalcitrant passengers. Perhaps his brain was overheated. Mine certainly felt like it, as again my seat caught the full force of the sun, but at least the young Japanese man next to me didn't want to talk. A familiar posse of taxidrivers at the bus station again assumed I would pay far too much for the short journey to my lodgings, but I was tired of being fleeced — it was like unlimited reruns of a bad movie. I waited, haggled over the fare, pretended to be patient and finally paid just a little too much.

The driver delivered me to the old Jewish quarter in the centre of the old town. A creaking gate set into a nondescript wall opened into a small, clean courtyard with a beautiful two-storey house set around three sides. Richly decorated with carved wooden panels, the house had tiny doorways and shuttered windows, and inside there were elegant floral designs painted directly onto the walls. My room led off a small tiled balcony on the second floor. It was tiny too, vivid with the colours of hand-embroidered cloths that covered my bed and curtained the wardrobe, and sitting awkwardly in the corner of the room, a television set and airconditioner looked incongruous. The bed had a soft but firm mattress, the television had satellite reception, and the BBC news — Russian president Yeltsin had just sacked another prime minister — and when I switched the airconditioner on, it made no noise. It was utter luxury.

Luxury or not, the lure of the streets pulled me out of my comfortable nest (where I'd fallen face-down on my bed, too exhausted to wash or unpack) and out into the brown city. After the sparkling luminosity of Samarkand's architecture, Bukhara's earth-toned buildings were easy on the eye, but no less splendid. One thousand years of history still stood in the old town, and away from the protected monuments people still went about their business with an apparent disregard for most of the trappings of the twentieth century. I walked up to the Labi Hauz, one of a few remaining large stone pools linked to the remnants of a once great canal system which watered the whole city until a century ago, when the Russians modernised the irrigation system. This was fortunate for the longevity of the residents of Bukhara, because the plague was a regular visitor to the city in the days when the pools were gathering places for people to wash and collect drinking water, or just sit and gossip.

The seventeenth-century Labi Hauz (a Tajik name meaning 'around the pool') still served as a gathering place. Men of all ages were gathered under the ancient mulberry trees drinking tea and talking, elderly grey-beards sat intently playing chess, and on the other side of the pool a tea-house served simple meals or simply tea. A few street-traders wandered around but lacked the 'hard sell' of the Samarkand hawkers, and on the edge of the canal close by, young boys stripped naked and dived into the water, waving furiously to whoever might be observing their acts of daring. I chose a seat next to the water, ordered tea and fell back into my seat with a sigh of relief. It was quiet except for the shrieking of the boys — it was peaceful, and it was beautiful. The late afternoon sun cast a golden light over the medressas and threw strong shadows into the arched portals and alleyways. I mentally calculated how many rolls of film I'd brought with me, knowing I'd soon be as busy with my camera as any tourist trying to capture the extraordinary shapes, lines and colours of this small city.

My friend in the Sydney cafe where I had cooked told me Bukhara was her favourite city. Looking at her photographs of narrow back streets and high walls of earth I'd felt nervous about being there on my own in such enclosed spaces, but after just a few days in the town I could see why she loved it. Early morning and late afternoon became my favourite times to explore the back streets. Sometimes I wandered quite aimlessly, but I always met someone, somewhere, who wanted to stop and talk or offer bottomless cups of tea as we sat on doorsteps or low walls in the shade. Most people were Tajik-speakers but Russian was a second language for many and, although it was not a favoured language, we could at least have limited conversations. The women would throw both hands up and exclaim with delight when they saw I was wearing the traditional loose dress and multi-patterned baggy pants, and my clothes were patted and tugged into place more times than I care to remember. I was delighted to find they were the coolest clothes I possessed, although I baulked at the idea of a headscarf as streetwear. If there was any breeze at all, I wanted my head to feel it. By the middle of the day I would be back in my tiny, low-ceilinged room, flat on my back with the airconditioner quietly humming, or sitting on the low wall in the courtyard below, paddling my feet in the puddles of water left lying on the hot tiles after the morning hosing.

Bukhara's marketplaces were full of traditional arts. In a communal arts centre where I'd enjoyed a fast game of table tennis with the best local player (a close match as it turned out) I watched a young man engaged in the painstaking task of embroidering with gold thread. I was told that before the revolution only men were allowed to embroider with gold thread — if women did, the gold would turn black. Why, I wasn't sure, although I imagined it had something to do with impurity, and couldn't bring myself to enquire further in case the answer had contemporary relevance. I liked watching this quietly industrious teenage boy so dextrous with a needle and thread. I filmed the Ikramov brothers, Sadullo and Sayfullo, at work in their blacksmith's workshop in Bukhara's old town, fashioning glittering knives and swords from dull metals that were heated to a white-gold glow and beaten into shape on an anvil in front of the furnace. The brothers worked as a team, their mallets rising and falling in an even, deafening rhythm. Great arcing showers of sparks flew off the stone grindstone as the knives were given their edge, the open window behind framing the sensuous shapes of the domes of a medressa. The work was dropped the instant a tourist group walked past, one of the brothers racing for the display cushion to stand politely in the doorway with his wares until they had either passed, or stopped to look. I often pondered on the apparent disinterest shown by many tourists I saw. There was often a rather glazed look about them that lacked the energy that curiosity can generate, yet here we were in one of the world's remote corners, with a cultural feast laid out, ready for us to take in our fill. Perhaps they were too hot, or simply did not have the appetite.

It was the embroidered *Suzana*, the Uzbek silk-on-cotton dowry needlework, that I fell hopelessly in love with. The ancient bazaars with their multi-domed roofs, designed to draw in and circulate air, were a welcome respite from the heat of the streets and drew me into their cool recesses on a daily search for the perfect *Suzana*. I knew I would recognise 'the one' when I saw it, but it had to be small enough to fit into my pack and suit my budget. I found it on my last day in Bukhara. A representation of the cosmos, it had a central mandala with lines radiating out to large, asymmetrical crosses, stitched on black fabric in bright, earthy primary colours contrasted with pale greens and white. It was unique, a simple, powerful pattern that seemed to speak of the fascination and yearning that humanity has for the mystery of the cosmos. But it seemed also that its maker, in her use of these earthy colours and large, bold symbols, had been able to communicate a sense of intimacy with her subject matter. It was compellingly attractive.

~

I didn't feel entirely comfortable in this country. It was as though the juice had been squeezed out of the people and I was spending my time among mostly inanimate monuments that spoke of nothing but an ancient history that had little relevance to daily life here. The summer fruit was ripe and luscious, the harvest and preparation of summer produce for the lean winter months was in full swing and the people were hospitable and friendly, but there seemed to be a greyness of spirit and underlying fear in them, as if they had to look over their shoulder before they made any sort of move. I had heard their Soviet-styled president was very controlling. An Uzbek man told me that his sister, who had fallen in love with a man from the Ukraine and had married him and gone there to live, was now divorced and back in Uzbekistan to be with her family. She was unable to get citizenship ('registration') again, even though she was born in Uzbekistan and her parents still lived there. She was not allowed to work, nor could she buy a house. People are unable to buy land, they can only buy buildings, and in Tashkent building values have plummeted. For example, a flat bought there four years ago for US$12,000 is now worth about US$4000.

My shopping successfully completed, I travelled from Bukhara to Khiva across the Kyzyl Kum Desert, in a car with two South Korean businessmen and their translator, a man from Tashkent. We were stopped three times by police for 'passport checks', a money-making venture I was told, whereby 'irregularities' in paperwork attract 'fines' which supplement the small salaries of the police. The Uzbek translator was resigned, but angry. It was a common occurrence he said, and they could do nothing about it. Issues of ethnicity also anger people, and create an underlying, simmering tension in many areas. In the 1920s Stalin redrew borderlines between Central Asian countries and placed several previously Tajik towns, Samarkand and Bukhara among them, in Uzbekistan. In 1924 the passports of these Tajik-speakers were stamped 'Uzbek', and to say you were other than this was a punishable offence. Chogyam Trungpa writes that 'When corruption enters a culture, it is because that culture ceases to be "now"; it becomes past and future.'[11] People travelled to Uzbekistan to see the past. The future was seen to be in a tightly controlled Islamic state — but the 'now' of the country seemed to exist in confusion, frustration and intolerance. If I needed a reminder of what Shambhala is *not*, then this was it.

There was just one guesthouse available to tourists in Khiva. The other was closed for restoration work. Upon my arrival the manager informed me that if a big group arrived I would be asked to leave my room, regardless of the booking Anya had made for me. I had no idea where he expected I would sleep, as all the other rooms were full, and I decided to stand my ground, insisting he telephone Anya and clear up the misunderstanding. The ensuing argument seemed to go on forever — I was glad I didn't understand the torrent of words as the manager threw himself around the little hallway, gesticulating wildly, his face working into a fantastic array of expression, but finally he gestured for me to speak with my 'travel agent'. She seemed bored, indifferent, suggested I go back to Urgench and stay in a hotel there, but I refused. Why would I stay in a dismal, grey Soviet town 35 kilometres away? Eventually I was given a small double room with a warning that someone might share it with me. 'Fine,' I said, but no one arrived. The drains smelled very bad so I draped a towel over the lidless lavatory and tried to drag the bathroom door shut. At midnight the electricity was shut off, the ceiling fan slowly rotated to a stop and the only window stuck fast. I slept very badly.

I was starting to feel exhausted even contemplating

filming in any more markets or museum monuments. Although the adults I met were generally friendly, I was beginning to be harassed by groups of small boys whose behaviour was aggressive, angry and demanding. Arriving en masse they would either stand in front of the lens, spoiling any sequence I was trying to shoot, or try to push me out of the way to get behind the camera. There was no sense of playfulness in these acts. Sometimes a passing adult, witnessing the disturbance, dispersed them with much shouting and waving of arms but in Khiva it was impossible to be free of them. The historic heart of Khiva has been preserved in its entirety and as a result its streets, alleyways and courtyards are almost empty except for tourists, and tourists were fair game for the small boys. However hard I tried, I couldn't hide from them. I crouched behind the walls of mausoleums to draw, tried to film myself drawing until a small hand shot out from behind the wall to grab the camera. I spent hours inside monuments that had paid entry just to get away from them. Where I wandered, they followed. I wanted to yell, 'I'm not a money machine, leave me alone!' but if they'd understood me, would they have cared? The heat was enervating, my hip and knee hurt viciously and I longed to be back in the mountains.

I had been in Uzbekistan just two weeks, but my visa conditions were set in concrete — two weeks and not a moment more, although I'd already decided it was quite long enough. Leaving Khiva bathed in a searing 50°C heat, I returned to Tashkent and went back through the border post, to be confronted by almost a kilometre of parked buses, all going to Almaty in Kazakstan, and all leaving at about the same time. I chose a bus at random, and climbed on board.

The Long Way Home

The trip from Tashkent was uneventful until we reached the dry steppe country, where we pulled off the road for *benzin* (petrol). The *benzin* was pumped straight from a truck parked up beside a tiny shack, the office, but it seemed there was a dispute between our bus 'hostess' and the *benzin* server over the price of our fuel. The ensuing screaming match continued for half an hour while we waited in the sweltering heat of the bus, sweat running down our faces as the passengers became more and more disgruntled and the fight turned physical, with unseen objects heard crashing into the walls of the shack. Finally we left. The dispute was still unsettled. Other buses passed us on the road. We were stopped at nearly every police checkpoint — with their minimum wage at around $4 a month, it seemed the local people had to make a living somehow. Our driver became increasingly irritated, although it was the hapless hostess who had to deal with the police graft. At about 2.30 am I heard a loud bang and the bus ground to a halt. A tyre had blown. I tried to get some rest in the hour it took to get the wheel-nuts off, and with the spare wheel eventually in place we lumbered on into the night. But there was still something wrong, the lumbering turned into a limp with unusual grinding noises coming from under the bus. As we went through yet another police checkpoint, the by now inevitable whistle was blown by the policeman on the barrier, the fluorescent baton was waved to flag us down, and the driver's face became very grim. He ignored them. A frantic activity of whistle blowing and baton waving followed, but the driver looked straight ahead and went on. The absurdity of the situation suddenly struck me and I hid my face in my sleeping bag as I shook with laughter. At least we'd had dinner.

For several hours we drove on at about 50 kilometres an hour, so slowly I wouldn't have been surprised to see donkey carts pass us as the dawn lit a beautiful, still morning, but at 8.30 am huge clouds of black smoke billowed up from under the bus and we ground to a halt. The driver seemed close to tears. I was asked to translate two tags that were attached to parts of the engine, but they were in German and I couldn't help. I sat with the women on the grass verge, writing my journal, filming and enjoying the cool early morning air as the men tinkered with the insides of the bus. What should have been a nine-hour journey had turned into a 24 hour exercise in patience and good humour, and light-hearted good humour had indeed prevailed, at least among the passengers. The bus was repaired, no one complained and we arrived in Almaty in time for lunch.

I picked up the rest of my belongings from Ziba, returned her Margaret Atwood novel (having devoured it in two days) and pushed on, into Kyrgyzstan. I felt as though I was well and truly on my way home now, but there were still challenges to face. In Bishkek, the capital of Kyrgyzstan, my focus would be on the paperwork necessary to cross the Torugart Pass, another notoriously difficult border crossing, this time over the Tian Shan mountains into the Xinjiang Province of China. I knew this would not be an easy trip. It's 700 kilometres from Bishkek to Kashgar in Xinjiang, and even with the right paperwork it is never certain that individual travellers will make it past corrupt officials with their hands out for extra cash, or even that transport and drivers will be reliable. Travellers have often been turned back for not having the right documents, and technically speaking, the border is open only to citizens of Kyrgyzstan and the People's Republic of China. It may be pure myth, but I heard even the American Ambassador once got turned back! Nevertheless I was determined to make this border crossing. It's probably the grandest, the most beautiful and certainly the most exciting route into or out of Central Asia.

In Bishkek I stayed with the wife of the optometrist I'd met in Almaty, and their two children. As Omar had promised, the flat was in the middle of town, a stone's throw from the pink OVIR registration building and the airconditioned Internet cafe — both locations of some importance. Nasrin, his wife, was very welcoming and sent the kids down to the department store to buy a thin foam mattress for me to sleep on. The recently purchased flat was almost devoid of furniture and at mealtimes we picnicked on the floor around a tablecloth laden with Nasrin's delicious Iranian dishes. Food in Uzbekistan had been largely uninspiring apart from the summer fruits — flat breads that were thick and rather tough, meat stews, noodle dishes, and *plov*. *Plov* was like a heavy rice pilaf and always smelt of mutton fat, but occasionally it was redeemed by the inclusion of a bulb of roasted garlic, so soft I could squeeze each clove to a husk and stir the creamy flesh through the rice to obliterate the fatty sheep smell. Nasrin's Persian curries and accompaniments were on a different plane altogether; I tried not to appear too greedy, but knew I would not eat as well as this again for some time.

Bishkek is a pretty town, backed by a high mountain range, an arm of the Tian Shan mountains, and since 1926 it has been Kyrgyzstan's capital. It's also a town devoid of ancient monuments, although Lenin with overcoat flapping still gestures grandly towards the mountains from his safe spot on the central square. The 'architecture' that draws people to Kyrgyzstan is the creative genius of nature, not humankind: the lofty, dramatic landscapes of the central Tian Shan and Pamir Alay ranges, softened by alpine lakes and cut through by hundreds of glaciers. This is a climber's paradise. I had no illusions about my ability to climb in the mountains, although my yearning to do so was deep and intense. It was painful to realise I couldn't experience the sublime landscapes I'd heard so much about, but I would concentrate instead on the crossing into China via the Torugart Pass, and enjoy my encounter with this special range of mountains from the comfort of a vehicle.

I discovered a Chinese company ran a sleeper bus over the pass, but there was a Catch-22 element to their operation — if you didn't have a Chinese visa that allowed entry over the pass, you couldn't get the 'Special Permission' that all foreigners must have to cross over. If you didn't have the 'Special Permission' paper, it was likely that your visa would be stamped 'Not Good for the Torugart Pass'. Furthermore, the bus made a night crossing — there would be no view of the mountains, and there was a strong possibility that I would be told to leave the bus at the Kyrgyz border post as the bus is not supposed to carry foreigners over the border zone itself. It most certainly didn't make a detour into the valley of Tash Rabat where a fifteenth-century *caravanserai* (an ancient travellers' inn) is built into the hillside. Travel companies sometimes had small groups going through but at US$400–500 it wasn't an option. I had just cashed my last traveller's cheque.

All of these deliberations were set aside when I discovered that the Chinese Embassy was closed for a week. The Shanghai Five — the Kazak, Tajik and Kyrgyz presidents, the Chinese Premier, and the Russian President Boris Yeltsin — were in town and security was suddenly very tight. The Shanghai Five was created in 1996 to resolve border issues between the republics of the former Soviet Union and China. Issues of regional security, settlement of the Afghan conflict and fighting the illegal trade of weapons and drugs in Central Asia were also on the agenda. Unaware of this top-security visit, I was in the building next to Bishkek's biggest hotel when police suddenly stopped me — no one was allowed to leave the room. A cavalcade of white-shirted men in black cars circled towards the hotel to my right, hundreds of police lined the road and the doors to the building were firmly locked. An hour passed before I was let out of the building to catch the bus back to the city centre, but the buses weren't allowed to leave. I sat with the trolleybus drivers in the shade for a few hours, contemplating the best course of action — once I was allowed back into town. I now had an extra week up my sleeve and one of my options was to fly west to Osh, a former Silk Road town at the western end of the agriculturally rich Ferghana Valley in Kyrgyzstan. Once there I would try and find a vehicle that was driving back to Bishkek. I had been told this road passed through some of the most spectacular landscapes in Kyrgyzstan, and that it was impossible to get a regular bus all the way through from Osh to Bishkek.

An Interlude

That night I had a dream about my mother. She was dressed up, what she would have called 'to the nines', with a swept-up hair style, and she walked with a sassy sway. She looked younger and slimmer than when I'd seen her last. She was going somewhere important and I needed to say goodbye, but there were some obstacles to overcome before I could be with her. I reached her at the last minute but it wasn't an emotional farewell, just a 'bye-bye' sort of occasion. I wondered if there was still some travelling to do in my relationship with her, or did it mean that in overcoming the obstacles, in the casual goodbyes, the relationship had travelled its distance? The feelings the dream left behind were light, and comfortable. I felt alright.

The airport was packed with brightly dressed women and children carrying huge plaid nylon bags. A young man called Tarr, pronounced as a purr, helped me drag my bags upstairs for ticket inspection, downstairs for bag inspection, and out to the plane to have them dumped unceremoniously into a cavity at the back of the aircraft. Tarr said the women and children were refugees from the 'Tajik conflict' and were returning home, but he didn't elaborate further. From Osh he was travelling on to Jalal-Abad, a resort town near the Uzbek border where multitudes of mineral springs bubble up in the foothills of the Ferghana range. It seemed a demographically confused area. While Osh is Kyrgyzstan's second biggest city, it has a predominantly Uzbek population which has been divided off by an arbitrary boundary drawn by the Soviets. The people of Jalal-Abad are also bilingual — speaking both Kyrgyz and Uzbek.

As the small plane taxied into the airport at Osh I turned to Tarr sitting beside me and asked, impulsively, if he would mind sharing his taxi to Jalal-Abad with me. I had a feeling of disquiet about Osh, although I wasn't to find out exactly what might have prompted this feeling until a few days later when I was comfortably ensconced in a *turbaza* (a summer holiday camp) in the mountains above Jalal-Abad. At the airport terminal Tarr negotiated for a taxi to take us across the tiny, narrow neck of land that is Uzbekistan. The customs officials, hot and bored, were disinterested in the contents of my pack after the first layer of dirty clothes had been inspected, and soon we were at the bus station in Jalal-Abad.

Arslanbob lies on the south-west slopes of the Ferghana range, 180 kilometres from Osh. It's famous for its groves of ancient walnut trees, and at over 3000 metres the mountain air is refreshingly cool while the valleys swelter. Tarr put me onto the Arslanbob bus and before nightfall I was in the village square watching the end of the day's trading and engaging in very limited conversations with the local people. Not many people spoke Russian. A chair was brought out for me and a bottle of Sprite propped into a fast-flowing creek to cool before I drank it. I had been the object of much curiosity on the journey up. It was a small, rounded bus, packed with people and goods, my seat in the aisle was a bag of grain, and an unseen kitten was mewing near me in someone's bag. Most women cradled babies or small children and large shopping bags, and took the seats; the men crowded into the aisles, squatting on bags of flour and other comfortable grocery items, or sitting on the luggage at the back. I was among the same riot of colour I'd seen everywhere in Uzbekistan — the bright trousers, patterned dresses and headscarves and a kind of hat I hadn't seen before — a tall, white conical felt hat the men wore perched on their heads.

At an unscheduled stop beside a stream, I took the camera out to film the bus against the backdrop of mountains. Two men who had been watching me closely in the bus approached and spoke what was obviously the only word of English they knew, 'police'. My heart sank, momentarily. I'd read the lengthy passage in the guidebook describing the corrupt practices of the Kyrgyz *militsia* but so far had encountered no problems, here or anywhere in Central Asia. Surely I wasn't going to be interrogated or subjected to demands for money on this friendly little bus in the middle of nowhere? By now everyone was out of the bus, sitting beside the creek, watching the interchange with interest. I composed myself, no need for reaction because nothing had happened — my mind was simply running with possibilities, but I could just as easily turn the situation around. I smiled, a big smile, flung my arm in the general direction of the landscape and said, '*Ya Christina, ya iz afstralii. Kyrgyzstan eta fkusna!*' (I'm Christina, I'm from Australia. Kyrgyzstan is delicious.) Everyone laughed, the two policemen looked at each other and roared with laughter, slapping their thighs and doubling up, and the tense moment disappeared. We climbed back onto our grain sacks in the aisle, I kept the camera out and made sure that no baby was left unfilmed.

The bus stopped in the main square of Arslanbob where a large statue of a lion looked out across the valley. Arslan is Muhammad's lion, his right-hand man who brought Islam to this region and is supposed to have died in the village. Legend has it that Arslan climbed to the top of a high mountain and threw walnut seeds down into this area, but another story has it that Alexander the Great brought a walnut from Greece and planted the first tree. The village houses of timber and yellow mud-brick had steeply pitched roofs typical of alpine architecture. Large gardens were bursting with flowers and vegetables, and over the laneways the foliage of the walnut trees hung creating cool avenues that crisscrossed the steep hillside. A big, roaring stream came crashing down the hill past a tea-house where old men with long white beards and tall white hats sat on an open verandah, and disappeared under the main square to go leaping off down beside the main road to the valley below. Donkeys were the major form of transport around the village for the menfolk and boys, and for carrying goods to and from the marketplace next to the main square. Further up the hill was the rustic Turbaza Arslanbob, a favourite summer camp for Central Asian holiday-makers, and my destination. Its spartan cabins were scattered over 29 hectares of wooded grounds; and trails in the hills led to waterfalls, caves and a small lake. A cavernous dining hall served plain Uzbek food and, tucked at the back of the communal shower and toilet block, was a sauna room. It was so hot in this sauna that my earrings burnt my ears.

I shared my cabin with a missionary couple who were working in Bishkek, their daughter, and their driver Gulam and his two children. Gulam was a great cook — he had won a recent cooking competition in Osh and made the best *plov* I had eaten (though it still couldn't match Nasrin's curry). From them I discovered why people immediately ask how old I am — age is so respected they need to know straight away where to place you in the social hierarchy, and I had thought it was a question born of curiosity! And most importantly, I found out that clashes between rebels and government troops in the Batken District, of which Osh is the centre, had resulted in hostages being taken — some of them foreign. My intuition had served me well. The official line was that the rebels were fundamentalist Muslims, but it was reported in the Bishkek English newspaper that in the opinion of officers from the Ministry of National Security, the burning of two villages, the capture of hostages and the demands for the release of members of the Uzbek Islamic Movement in exchange for hostages was simply a diversionary tactic. They saw these acts as a test of the Kyrgyz army and the effectiveness of border controls, by a group headed by a man who had become 'famous' for robberies on Uzbek passenger trains. But Uzbekistan feared terrorist attacks, and quickly closed its borders to all non-Uzbek citizens. Getting back to Osh, the nearest airport, required crossing Uzbek borders twice. My options for returning to Bishkek were suddenly very limited.

My 'knights in shining armour' were two Swiss tourists who were travelling with three Kyrgyz men in a Russian four-wheel-drive van. Arslanbob was the start of a nine-day tour for the Swiss men, with Nikolai as their driver and cook, his son Dema as second driver, and a second Dema as German translator. They were headed into the far north-west of Kyrgyzstan, an area few tourists visit, camping most nights and relying on local markets for food. They were returning to Bishkek by the same route I had dreamed of travelling, not knowing then how I would accomplish it. I couldn't refuse their offer to accompany them. Actually it was Nikolai's offer, no doubt driven partly by financial interests, but it was a fair price and it didn't take long to convince the two Swiss men to share their holiday with an Australian woman. Driver Dema and I would leave the group at Lake Issy-Kul and return to Bishkek at the end of seven days, me to apply for an urgent visa for China, and he to return to university.

It was a long, absorbing journey. We crossed the top of the wide Ferghana Valley, the landsçape rich with scenes of the late-summer harvest. Large sunflower heads lay drying, spread out on the sides of roads and in courtyards, and stripped corncobs of red and yellow lay drying on rooftops. Fields were golden with uncut grasses, but it must have been time to gather in the hay as every morning we passed men on the road with scythes over their shoulders. Melon stalls lined the roadsides, and offered the three varieties I had enjoyed so much in Uzbekistan. I was told that in Soviet days this valley fed forty per cent of the Soviet population. It was a staggering thought. At the head of the valley the turquoise green Naryn River flowed big and sluggish, in spite of its weight of hydroelectric dams. We soon entered a barren, eroded landscape that reminded me of Arizona, complete with what looked like saltbush. A lovely scene in the midst of this rugged country stays in my mind. On a hillside in the middle of nowhere stood an ugly construction that looked like a large bus shelter, except that at its centre a fat pipe gushed water. A slatted seat ran around its edge. On it perched a small girl, combing her long hair and dangling her feet, her tiny figure contrasted against the huge harsh landscape. It was like a surrealist painting.

~

The Chatkal range is in the far north-west of Kyrgyzstan. Nikolai was taking us into the Sary Chelek Zapovednik (National Park) to see the lakes and walk in the national park. Here, bubbling mineral springs become the streams that feed the lake system from the surrounding canyons. Dema the driver knew lots of local creation myths. The story of Sary Chelek began at a time when the mountains and the water were at war with each other, but neither would give in. The water finally said, 'I can just rush away from you,' and the mountains replied, 'We can surround you, and imprison you.' I preferred Dema's alternate story that had the mountains surrounding the lakes to protect the villagers. We camped outside the national park perimeter, in a small gorge with big golden rocks and a fast river hissing under the cliffs. Spreading walnut trees and slender larches gave us shade, and donkeys grazed on the open, grassy flat. The evening's *chai* (tea) was flavoured with peppermint sage that Nikolai had picked at a mineral spring where we'd stopped to fill up our water bottles. In the evening we walked along the bottom of the gorge picking rosehips for breakfast *chai*, stopping at a pool in the river to wash away the dust of the day's journey. The water was surprisingly warm.

The national park is reached by traversing a steep pass — from here I could see the 4000-metre Talassky range peeping over the top of the Chatkal mountains. Just one month ago I had been in those mountains with Valodia, in another country, at the peak of summer. Now, most of the wildflowers had finished, their seed heads probably tucked into the small haystacks dotted everywhere through the lower mountains, even in the forest. Everywhere that grass could be cut and a scythe could be swung, there was a little haystack. Beside the lakes were orchards of wild cherry, and what looked like a small quince tree, the grass cut under these trees as well. People fished beside a notice that said 'No Fishing', and we were later invited to swim in Lake Sary Chelek where a notice proclaimed 'No Swimming — 100 som fine'. The water was cool and a deep turquoise. From where we stood on the bank it was clear enough to see a small water snake exploring the bottom of the inlet. Later, the snake swam across to the other side, its head held high above the water.

We crossed high mountain passes and drove through mighty gorges. The roads were often atrocious, but Nikolai drove with skill in conditions that ranged from fair to very bad, through some of the most rugged country I had seen in Central Asia. He cooked, shopped, packed, peeled potatoes, lit fires and provided a wealth of information about the country we passed through. His love for his country was very obvious. He had spent his childhood around Lake Issy-Kul (Warm Lake) in the east, but said that some of the places we were visiting were very special for him. The Talas Valley was one of these places. It sits comfortably between the Kyrgyz Alatau range and the Talassky Alatau range. If I had fired an arrow from horseback while I was on the high mountain trails with Valodia in the Talassky range, I could imagine it being carried on the wind over the mountain tops and down into the Talas Valley. It was a strange thought, that I was so close to Valodia, Vladimir and Zhenia in their Kazak village, and yet so distant.

Dema told me that in the fifth century BCE there was a great battle here in the valley between the Arabs and the Chinese. This happened after rain, and the whole valley was covered in the corpses of elephants (Chinese), camels (Arabic) and humans, all in thick mud. The Arabs won the battle for Kyrgyzstan, and Islam was established. Muslim pilgrims come to pray here, at the tomb of the legendary *khan* (ruler) Manas — at least, legend has assigned his tomb here. It's said he was born in Kyrgyzstan while his father was away fighting a battle in the Altai. A white eagle came to Manas' father in a dream, meaning that in nine months he would have a son. Manas had Mongol features, as the originally Siberian Kyrgyz and a Mongol tribe had already intermixed, but it's said also that the skeleton in this tomb is two and a half metres long — he was a great man indeed.

This ruler was the super-hero of the Manas epics, acclaimed as one of the finest epic traditions and the pinnacle of the Central Asian oral culture. Two and a half times longer than the *Mahabharata* of India and twenty times longer than the *Odyssey* of Greece, the epic tells the story of Manas and his exploits as he created a homeland for his people in the face of their adversaries. Traditionally, travelling epic storytellers brought this poetry to life in the felt tents of the nomads, in the bazaars and teahouses of the towns, reciting and improvising before enthusiastic audiences. The storytellers who sang the Manas epic were in a special category called *manaschis* — improvisation was the mark of a good *manashi*. That tradition is dead, but interest in the epic is growing again. For example, the Kyrgyz government and UNESCO declared 1995 to be 'The International Year of Manas' — locally, of course. And Kyrgyzstan's 'Eternal Legacy International Social Foundation' has launched an unprecedented project involving the publication of the epic in a volume, which, at four metres wide, promises to be the world's largest book.

I was more interested in the familiar-looking carved stone statues half hidden in the grass beside the Manas' tomb. Dema couldn't tell me exactly how old they were, just 'very old', but I had seen similar sculptures in Siberia, at Lake Baikal. And at the top of a hill near the tomb were the blue rags tied to sticks as prayers, as in Buryatia, Siberia. I loved these interconnections that point to humanity's links as a family with differences, but an underlying unity.

Karl and Rainer, quiet, serious men, kept very much to themselves. They were interested in the technical side of the landscape, in numbers and dates — what volume of water flowed through the dams, how high was this pass, when was this road built? It was Nikolai's job to provide all this information, and Dema's job to translate it into German, but this wasn't what interested me. I wanted to know about the people, their history and their culture, and fortunately Nikolai's son Dema spoke enough English to tell me the stories I wanted to hear. Nor, it seemed, were the two men interested in communicating with local people. We took turns to sit in the front seat of the van, the best place as far as I was concerned because I could manipulate the camera more easily and even recharge batteries in the sunlight, but it was also the most visible seat for anyone passing by, or standing at the road's edge. People waved often, especially children but the two German men remained impassive, upright in their seat, never even raising an arm in acknowledgement. I found such unfriendliness embarrassing and wondered what Nikolai made of it.

We sat down to a picnic beside a raging river on windswept, treeless ground. The last high pass was in front of us — it would be too cold to stop and eat lunch up there. A forlorn stray dog, a bitch feeding pups, came quietly by and sat down to see if food would come her way. Nikolai gave her bread and soup, the same as we'd had. Eagles and falcons were circling above the high rocks, but no other animals were in sight, nor were there any dwellings. I'd seen a few stray dogs in these mountains — skinny, slinking animals, withdrawn as if they knew they weren't going back to a life of barking and pats and regular dinner. This bitch with her pups was a sad sight and I was glad Nikolai hadn't chased her away.

~

I was dreaming vividly most nights. One dream had me in a small two-seater aeroplane with a man who instructed me to take off on a runway between some trees in the middle of a city. I tried to build up enough power for the takeoff, but I wasn't pressing my foot on the accelerator hard enough and couldn't get up enough speed. I turned the plane around to have another try, but became enmeshed in a strange configuration of roundabouts and one-way streets, travelling the wrong way. I wanted very much to fly the plane, but still couldn't achieve lift-off. It was a beautiful metaphor for my feelings about the film at this time, as I constantly questioned whether I had made the right choice to travel with these men. I didn't know what story I was telling here, which was the right direction, and I was so tired I felt permanently stale. Perhaps I should simply treat this time as a holiday?

Over the last pass we dropped down into the Suusamyr Valley on a new road, a dream with no potholes. Rumour had it that this road was a major artery for drugs smuggled from Afghanistan to Russia. At the end of the valley we stopped to watch a group of village women constructing a brightly coloured Kyrgyz carpet made from multiple layers of felt. The design is laid out in teased wool, then hot water is poured over the carpet and the fibres are condensed into thick felt by stamping on it. The man of the house invited us in for *chai*, but vodka was produced as well for toasts and food was laid out on the big carpet in the sparsely furnished main room of the house. I walked in after the men were seated and in my attempt to move to the only vacant position on the carpet, the farthest corner, made the *faux pas* of stepping in front of a male guest, my feet touching the carpet. I looked in horror at Nikolai, but he smiled kindly and gave a little shrug. The world wouldn't stop turning. I remembered Sainu's reaction two months before in a Mongolian *ger*, his anger and betrayal of our offensive behaviour to our hosts, and felt glad to be in Nikolai's company.

Our host said that had he known of our arrival, he would have prepared a sheep for us so I was pleased the visit had been a surprise — both for the family and for myself. A guest in a Muslim country is given an honoured position that I was just beginning to understand. Guests are treated with absolute courtesy and selflessness. The sacrifice of a sheep in this poor area would probably have been a significant drain on the family's resources, and to refuse to eat it would have insulted them. I had coped with diarrhoea (what I termed 'exploding bum syndrome') several times on this journey, and my stomach was feeling queasy even now. The prospect of breaking my thirty-year vegetarian diet with fatty mutton or perhaps the insides of a sheep's head didn't make me feel good. Our host made a moving toast to friendships and peace between countries and we left feeling warm and fuzzy, from the kindness and generosity as well as the vodka.

~

It was 31 August, Independence Day for Kyrgyzstan. Young children, many carrying flowers and wearing white shirts and black skirts or trousers, were out in the village streets. Horse and donkey carts were packed with cheerful people, and the streets were still colourful in the early morning sun with lines of bedding and carpets draped over fences for airing. It was my last day with my fellow travellers. At the top of the final pass a huge storm was brewing — the sky was an inky purple-black and there were brief periods of heavy rain and noisy thunder. Women were selling fish by the roadside. We must have been quite close to Song-Kul Lake that reputedly jumps with fish. This tiny jewel-like lake is set among lush high pastureland where herders bring their animals for the summer months, and part of a small zoological reserve where a diminishing number of wolves still roam. We were on our way to a town on the shores of Lake Issy-Kul to meet a Kyrgyz man who keeps two eagles he has raised from chicks. He hunts with the eagles, a traditional Kyrgyz occupation that is disappearing fast, but so is some of the prey that the eagles bring down, including animals as big as wolves.

Issy-Kul is a huge lake, 170 kilometres long and 70 kilometres across, in area the world's second-largest alpine lake after Lake Titicaca in South America. The lake never freezes due to a combination of thermal activity, mild salinity and extreme depth; and in summer the air is never hot and stifling as it was in Bishkek. Many peoples over the millennia have made this place their home. Various nomadic tribal cultures arriving in succession have left artefacts here — Neanderthal camps, petroglyphs carved on rock faces, ancient burial hills and even ruins of towns hidden beneath the lake's surface. The town we were visiting was well above ground on the lower slopes of the foothills, the mountain ranges behind hidden in heavy cloud. The rain had by now turned into a deluge, the roads flooded with muddy water. It was slow going.

The man who hunts with eagles was at home. His birds at the back of the house were making a huge din — a continuous, distracting noise. I wondered how the family could live with it, but it was probably like having aeroplanes flying over your house — you eventually got used to it. The birds don't hunt in the heat of summer. I guessed they would be a bit sluggish with the heat, but it was now late August and the season would be starting again in September. He had two birds, a three-year-old male who was making most of the noise, and a nine-year-old female, the smaller of the two but responsible for bringing down the two wolves whose skins we saw hanging in the guest yurt (the nomadic tent). The male bird had thicker legs and a greater wingspan than the female (his wings measured about two metres when fully extended), although their body size was similar. These were magnificent animals. Their owner had raised them from chicks, as it is vitally important to develop a good rapport with birds if they are to be your hunters. It was important for the whole family to establish this relationship. He demonstrated how a leather hood is slipped over the bird's head before the hunt, so it's not distracted before it pursues its prey, and I watched as he allowed the bird to take a good look at the hood before he gently drew it over its head. He was keen on the idea of a film about this tradition, from the raising of chicks to the hunt itself, and I saw how it could be expanded to bring in the Kazak tradition of hunting with falcons, still practised in the Altai area on the Mongolian side of the mountains, but this would be a long-term project and I wasn't sure I was the right person for the job.

~

It was time to make my farewells. Nikolai's son Dema and I had to get back to Bishkek, I had to begin my battle for the Torugart Pass. The week I had spent with these men had indeed been a real holiday, a chance to rest and draw breath before the next leg of the journey and I was grateful to them for the opportunity to see so much of the remote mountainous regions of Kyrgyzstan. I was especially appreciative of Nikolai's unflagging enthusiasm and hard work, and his gentleness. Nikolai communicated respect for others but was also gentle to himself, in spite of all his hard work, and it was an immensely endearing, attractive quality. I would miss him. But we had forgotten it was Independence Day. There were no buses — they were all in Bishkek waiting to bring people home from the celebrations — and no taxis. It was also pouring with rain again. There were people waiting, frustrated, at the bus stop so Nikolai decided to take us and others to the nearest big town where we could be sure of picking up a taxi. I liked the Central Asian taxis. Anyone with a car and the petrol could be a taxi, and as a potential customer you simply stood by the roadside, flagged a car down and negotiated a price. Ours was a Russian saloon from the 1960s, its driver a tall thin man in his late fifties, I guessed — a silent man with a permanent little smile playing around his lips. His head almost reached the roof of the car and he had an eagle tattooed on the back of his right hand. It was a quiet, comfortable journey.

The High Pass

I spent a frustrating week in Bishkek. The Chinese company whose sleeper bus made a weekly trip over the Torugart Pass also had some accommodation on the premises, so late that night, the streets surging with crowds on their way home from the Independence Day celebrations, I was dropped off at the company's compound near the railway line. The fireworks had just finished, drunken men and women lurched along the footpaths and the compound was very dark. I felt a prickle of unease. Chogyam Trungpa writes that 'True fearlessness is not the reduction of fear, but going beyond fear' and that 'Going beyond fear begins when we examine our fear: our anxiety, nervousness, concern and restlessness.'[12] I stood quite still and listened, to my surroundings and to the thoughts yapping like a dog in my head. But that's all these thoughts were, the mindless yappings of an irritated dog, a reaction to the sudden feelings of displacement from gentle countryside to the mayhem of a city, many of whose inhabitants had too much alcohol under their belts. I walked through the gates into the compound to find the man with the room keys.

They wanted US$5 for the room. It was disgusting, with filthy lumpy mattresses heaped on top of two rusty iron beds, no windows, no other furniture and a nasty smell. When I complained I was shown the only other room, a disused storeroom with two hard beds in it, no ventilation and the electrical wiring for the light switch hanging out of the wall. In its early days the compound had been a kindergarten. Here in the storeroom the walls were decorated with dusty, torn friezes of cute Disneyesque animals, leaving a bizarre impression of kindliness and softness. I gave in, rather ungraciously, took the storeroom and tried to sleep on the achingly hard bed.

I had been relying on these people to get me the documentation for the Torugart Pass, but the night's accommodation and the attitude of those who rented it to me had left a nasty taste in my mouth. Next day I walked up to the Chinese Consulate to apply for an urgent visa, mentioning that I wanted to enter via the Torugart Pass. 'Ready on Monday,' she said. A Kyrgyz travel agent found a flat for me to rent — a bright, airy, plainly furnished seventh-floor apartment with views across to the mountains where I could cook, sleep in comfort, dance if I had the energy, read until all hours, whatever I liked, for US$7.50 per night. The flat belonged to a young, single mother with a small baby whose mother Nina lived in the apartment block next door. Tanya and the baby stayed with her mother while I was renting her flat. I was pleased to be providing a little extra income for Tanya, and they seemed pleased to have me there, especially Nina. I was invited for breakfast, lunch and dinner. Nina cooked delicious Russian-style soups, pancakes, pastries and sweets, and I was treated to a hot bath — a luxury because the city hadn't had hot water for a good part of the summer, and still didn't have it. As in Mongolia and Kazakstan, the Russian-built system of water pipes under the city was in serious disrepair and summer was the best time to replace them, but doing this left the entire city without an amenity I simply took for granted at home. Nina boiled up great pots of water on the stove, the bath was deep and hot and I lay in there until my skin wrinkled like a prune.

The Chinese company had indeed purchased the Special Permit I needed to cross the Torugart Pass, but wouldn't give it to me until they saw the Chinese visa stamped in my passport, although I had paid for the permit in advance. The Chinese Consulate wouldn't give me a visa stamped 'Good for the Torugart Pass' because I couldn't show a Special Permit. I had arranged to travel over the pass with another Swiss couple, a man and wife in their thirties, and an Irish woman, with a car and Kyrgyz driver booked for Wednesday 8 September. On Monday, my hopes high, I went to the consulate to pick up my visa as promised, to be told 'Not ready, come back Wednesday.' The Irish woman, also waiting to pick up her passport, had been told to come back next week although her application had gone in a week before mine. I wondered how much satisfaction the staff got from playing these controlling games. We stood our ground, we begged, we pleaded, we waited, and waited. Finally our passports were placed on a desk, papers were filled out and the magic visa stamps appeared. I had to keep my mouth firmly shut, wanting to cry out 'Please, please make it "Good for the Torugart Pass!"' The stamp came down with a bang, the deed was done, and I said quietly 'This is good for the Torugart Pass, yes?' 'No!' 'But,' I said in desperation, 'this is the way I'm going to China, tomorrow. My transport is paid for.' 'You have no permission to go this way.' 'Yes I do,' I said, 'it's with the Chinese travel company.' 'Well, maybe it's good, maybe it's not, maybe you get through, and maybe you don't. You have no

Special Permission.' 'Yes, yes I do, can you telephone them?' 'Absolutely impossible.' End of story. The Irish woman was given her passport, but the rules for payment had suddenly changed and she was charged double the usual amount. But at least she had been able to present her Special Permission paper and so was theoretically eligible to cross the pass. We fled the consulate building and dropped into a seat in the nearest bar, ordered a beer and compared passports, scrutinising the Chinese characters on our visa stamps. There seemed to be no difference.

We were nervous, but in good spirits. We had done better than several other independent travellers we had met; we hadn't been refused visas outright. I had heard there was already snow on the pass. The mountains behind Bishkek were wearing their first thick mantle, looking absolutely beautiful in the early morning light. We had been assured by the Chinese company that both car and driver were reliable, and although the driver had started making unreasonable demands for extra money before we'd even left the city, the landscape in front of us, bathed in bright autumn sunshine, quickly lifted our spirits.

Torugart is a high, remote outpost, 540 kilometres from Bishkek and 180 kilometres from Kashgar in China, with difficult roads on both sides of the border. Most people make an overnight stop at Naryn, a rather bleak town with a big military presence, but with a few places to stay for travellers who are making their way over the pass. Our driver wouldn't take us to the cheap hotel as we'd planned; we were to stay in his apartment, a second-floor three-roomed flat in one of the anonymous apartment blocks that seemed to be a signature of Russian occupation, that I'd seen all over Central Asia. He left us there, and disappeared to complete his registration papers, necessary for crossing the no-man's-land of the pass. He arrived back after dark to start cooking our dinner. It was a good dinner and we ate it very late that night. Knowing we had to be up at 4.00 am, this and his rather autocratic manner didn't endear him to me. The following morning he simply added the cost of our food and (pricey) accommodation onto the extras that slipped into the conversation as we drew near to the first checkpoint. We had negotiated to make a brief stop at the ancient *caravanserai* (travellers' inn) on a tenth-century Silk Road site, fifteen kilometres off the road before the checkpoint, arriving there at sunrise through the narrow valley of Tash Rabat where beautiful rock walls opened out into a small basin. The stone building with its central domed room was nestled into the velvety hillside. The rising sun threw long shadows of its uniquely Central Asian outline onto the floor of the basin. Several yurts were dotted across the green valley, and smoke from breakfast fires drifted up and curled over the little valley. It was very quiet, and utterly beautiful.

At the outer gate of the border post we had to show our passports, and the driver started demanding more money, for the car, he said. We had paid the Chinese company in full for the trip, including his wage, vehicle expenses and the bribes for the guards, and paid also for the detour to the *caravanserai*, but it looked as if we were about to be forced to hand over a lot more. The Swiss couple were by now so nervous their voices were shaking as we discussed in low tones how to explain to him that we had paid him in full for the journey, plus his added expenses for food and accommodation. I was the only passenger who spoke enough Russian to explain it to him. On the dusty high desert road we pulled over and hammered out a solution over the bonnet of his car. He was angry, I was adamant, but finally we both yielded and reached a compromise. I stuffed the last of my dollars into my brassiere and hoped the border guards would be happy with the money they were about to receive.

In the small customs office at the Kyrgyz border, a desolate and windswept place, the large officer at the desk withheld our passports and demanded we each pay him US$20. I told him the driver had our money for him, but the driver had mysteriously disappeared. I knew without a doubt I could not afford to be afraid or angry — I had observed too often how easy it is to make an unpleasant situation worse by being overcome with these strong emotions. There were a tense few minutes while the driver was found and brought into the office, only to hand over three fifty-som notes (about US$15). We had paid him three times that amount for the guards! I kept my mouth shut, hoping he'd have to hand over the rest of the money on his way back through the post. At 11.15 am we were through and ready to drive the final twelve kilometres over no-man's-land to the border with China where we were to be met by a driver who was coming from Kashgar to pick us up. It was a complicated arrangement. Kyrgyz border officials insisted on written confirmation of onward transportation into China, and if that means of transport did not arrive to meet you at the border on the nominated day, you would be detained and turned back.

Our driver dropped us at the large gate separating China from Kyrgyzstan, unloaded our bags, turned the car around and left, his pockets full of our money. There was no one there to meet us. On the Chinese side, two soldiers sat in the sun on low stools at the front of a small compound, eating their lunch. Behind the compound, Chinese characters, metres high, stretched across the hilltop. On the Kyrgyz side, still our side, two soldiers in a tiny hut gestured with their rifles for us to stay where we had landed, right beside the gate. We decided to make a picnic with the last of our food, it had been a long time since breakfast at the driver's house, and we also decided not to panic.

It was a great decision. It's so much more dramatic and convincing to believe that all things happen to us rather than observe how we make them happen. To panic in this place, at this time, might have landed us squarely back in Bishkek with considerably less money. We ate all our food, sat in the sun and tried to make light of our situation.

An hour later our jeep arrived. We were elated — we hadn't been forgotten! But the driver had with him the list of people who had the Special Permits needed for the Chinese side, and the Irish woman wasn't on the list. Anxiety crept in again as we loaded up the jeep and drove down to the Chinese Customs and Immigration compound at the bottom of the hill, where we unloaded our bags once more, feeling our self-congratulations had been premature. A group of very young Chinese frontier police and a friendly soldier stood around and looked at the bags, showing little interest in them and preferring instead to talk to us. Their captain spoke perfect English. A tall, good-looking, courteous man, he was everything I didn't expect in a frontier policeman, but he said he liked his job, he met interesting people and he wasn't married so this remote outpost suited him very well. His men, who looked like teenagers, milled around singing and laughing, giving us shy glances, and one even danced out of the office door after taking a cursory look at our hand luggage. It was the strangest police force I had ever come across, and the most delightful. The captain was apologetic about the Special Permit papers, saying there was a problem with the date of entry for the Irish woman, but we could wait there until he had made a phone call to the last Chinese customs and immigration post, or just drive down there and try our luck. We elected to wait, and it wasn't long before he came back to tell us it had been sorted out. Like Nikolai, who had worked so hard to give me and the Swiss tourists the very best Kyrgyz experience he could, this man was a gentleman.

Kashgar

I soon realised how very lucky I had been to make it through the pass. One month before, the worst flooding this area had experienced in a hundred years had ravaged the valley below the mountain. Raging torrents took large areas out of the roadway and tore causeways apart, dumping enormous piles of stones and rubble across the track. Two weeks ago the road had been impassable. The landscape contrasted starkly with the Kyrgyz side of the mountain range — it was treeless, desolate, significantly drier, with low mountains eroded into surreal shapes and red-walled canyons crumbling into the riverbeds below. It looked breathtaking in the late afternoon sunshine, but I was pleased I was only passing through.

Kashgar was noisy. I had forgotten about the incessant horn tooting in China, but the busy streets packed with bicycles, motorbikes and horse and donkey carts were pleasant to explore without the high levels of pollution I had experienced in other Chinese towns. Kashgar has existed as a settlement for at least 2000 years. It had been an important market town on the Silk Road where caravans from China, the camels laden with raw silk, could rest after the rigours of the desert crossing. Whether the crossing was north or south of the Taklamakan and Lop deserts, it was still roughly 1,200 kilometres of extreme danger from fierce winds that covered tracks, and icy conditions in winter and searing heat in summer. Many caravans did not reach their destination, having wandered off course and disappeared into the shifting sands. The Turki word *Taklamakan* means 'go in and you won't come out', but fortunately most people did survive. They packed the silk onto horses in Kashgar and finally onto yaks, and crossed the icy passes of the Pamirs or the Karakoram mountains to reach their final, faraway destinations. The soft texture and beauty of silk fabric made it a particularly popular commodity with the Romans, who saw the trade route to the East as a route for silk rather than the other goods that were traded. It wasn't until the nineteenth century, however, that the term 'Silk Road' was coined, by a German scholar.

These days Kashgar keeps some of its heady mix of ancient cultures, and it is still an oasis town. Fed by streams from the Tian Shan mountains and irrigated by canals and ditches that are a legacy of ancient Uyghur cultivation methods, the surrounding land produces abundant amounts of fruit, cotton, wheat, maize and rice. But a huge statue of Mao Zedong on the edge of the People's park, unattractive high-rise buildings and new department stores along wide sealed roads are evidence of a Chinese remaking of the town. And it's not just the town that is being refashioned, as China floods the region with Han Chinese immigrants, diluting the original Uyghur population and quelling any eruption of Uyghur nationalism. The Uyghur civilisation has an extraordinary history. Powerful and prestigious, it dominated Central Asia for more than a thousand years but now, having declined steeply during the rule of the Nationalist Chinese, it's a culture in danger of extinction under Chinese Communist rule.

The Uyghur people are of a mixed Turkic–Mongol heritage. By the middle of the eighth century Uyghur rule, issuing from its capital in northern Mongolia, had extended to Lake Baikal in the north, and south to India and to China. They were a united, strong nation, and during this time were developing the seeds of the advanced culture which characterised the Uyghurs of later ages. By the beginning of the ninth century the state was disintegrating. The Uyghurs fell out with their powerful Kyrgyz neighbours (another Turkic people) and, driven from their traditional grazing grounds, they swept south and west. Three separate Uyghur kingdoms were finally established — one in today's Gansu Province of China, with Dunhuang as its centre; one in northern Xinjiang Province near the present-day town of Turpan; and the third at Kashgar. Originally the religious beliefs of these people, like those of their Siberian and Mongolian neighbours, were shamanistic, but as they moved south they adopted first Manichaeism (a Persian faith based on the opposition of the spirit and the flesh), then Buddhism and finally, in 934, the Uyghurs of Kashgar adopted Islam. Almost three hundred mosques were built in Kashgar, and eighteen Islamic schools educated up to 2000 students in any given year in subjects such as arithmetic, geometry, astronomy, medicine, agriculture; and of course in reading, writing and Islam. A fifteenth-century library had a collection of about 200,000 books. The Uyghurs who had settled in Dunhuang, however, remained Buddhist.

At the end of the fourteenth century the Islamic and Buddhist kingdoms merged into one great state, maintaining their independence until the Manchus, who set up a huge empire in China, invaded and conquered the

Uyghurs in 1759. The Uyghur people revolted many times against Manchu rule, successfully expelling the Manchus a hundred years later. By this time Great Britain was so fearful of Russian expansion into the area that it bankrolled another, successful, Manchu invasion. In 1884 the area was renamed Xinjiang, meaning 'new territory', and annexed into the Manchu empire. In 1911 the Nationalist Chinese overthrew Manchu rule establishing a republic, and in 1949 the Uyghurs fell under Communist Chinese rule when the Nationalists were defeated.

It wasn't until the end of the nineteenth century that the Western world began to have some understanding of the very high degree of civilisation the Uyghur kingdom had reached. The same explorers and archaeologists who had plundered the caves of Dunhuang, where I had stood in wonder in front of some of the most beautiful frescoes I had ever seen, had carried off literally tons of artefacts from these and other cave temples and monastery ruins in the far west of China. They brought to the West relics of a rich Uyghur culture detailed in manuscripts, wall paintings, statues, documents and books. Some of the explorers who wrote of these finds in the early twentieth century were convinced the Uyghur language and script was a source of enrichment for other Central Asian civilisations, and that the Uyghurs knew how to print books centuries before Gutenberg invented his press. When compared with

European farmers of the same period, the Uyghurs appear to have had a far more advanced society. Documents discovered in this area showed that an Uyghur farmer was capable of writing a contract using legal terms. The Mongols and Manchus used the Uyghur script for almost 800 years too, and the Uyghurs emerged as teachers of royalty, ambassadors, governors, scholars and military officers, across Central Asia.

I was intrigued to discover I had travelled around the edges of the ancient Uyghur empire in my journey to find Shambhala. My first travels out into the western deserts of China took me to the eastern edges of this empire, where I had been so entranced by the Buddhist art of the Wei people, an art that the Uyghur rulers of the Wei were responsible for encouraging throughout northern China. And then I travelled to Mongolia, where the empire stretched to the Altai mountains. After reaching the northern extent of the Uyghur empire at Lake Baikal, I had gone into the Altai, to Mount Belukha. And then to Kyrgyzstan, in the Talas Valley where Dema told me the story about the great battle in the mud, the Uyghurs had fought with the Arabs and the Tibetans against the Chinese. Now I was in Kashgar, a later Uyghur capital where the indigenous people still make up a large percentage of the population.

Traditional Uyghur medicine can be traced back through written records for more than 2700 years. It was

an Uyghur man, Talat, who took me to see a shaman in the old town, to find a remedy for my aching knees and hip. He was a self-confident, self-appointed guide who had hailed me from a cafe table on the footpath: 'Hello! Welcome to Kashgar!' I was glad to meet him. Most Uyghur people seemed quite reserved, and not interested in communicating with a Western woman tourist, but Talat was both businessman and guide. He was an intelligent man with a good command of English, and was willing to appear on camera. He took me to an unpaved street where the fine grey dust that I'd come to associate with Kashgar puffed up around my shoes with every step I took. The street was busy with shoppers and hawkers. It was too narrow for donkey carts, but there was enough noise and activity, including motorbikes ducking and weaving around the pedestrians, to create bedlam.

The shaman was kneeling in a narrow recessed doorway that was painted bright red and lodged between two shops in the old town. He seemed oblivious to the hubbub in front of him. Above his head, swaying in the light breeze, were hung bundles of dried frogs, lizards and other small animals that I couldn't identify, and on the shelf behind him sat jars containing thick dark masses of worm-like creatures. He wore a brown jacket, a round brown cap, his beard was streaked with grey, and he seemed no different from any man I might meet in the street here.

Strangely, he placed a pink plastic bag over my wrist before he took my pulse. Talat translated. I was unpeaceful in my heart sometimes, he said, my knees, and the back of my neck were problem areas, my kidneys were unbalanced. I wanted to show him the size of my backpack, for him to feel the weight of it, show him a map of the distances I'd covered. These were defensive thoughts. He gave me herbs to take, a thick brown cake that looked like a large block of hashish, saying that after forty days of taking these I would be 'super-powered'. I truly hoped so, but I hoped also that my medicine didn't contain any of the dried wildlife I'd seen hanging above my head. He also warned against two of the things I had been most enjoying in this searing summer heat — cold beer, and any other food or drink straight from the refrigerator. I had noticed that alcohol adversely affected my knees, and I guessed ice-cream was also in this category. I had become an ice-cream-a-day sort of woman, as it was too hot to eat anything else most of the time. Certainly my knees grew stronger over the next few weeks, but I was reluctant to take the strange looking medicine through Australian customs and immigration, so I did not get to achieve the 'super-powered' state promised to me after taking the herbs for forty days.

Like most travellers to Kashgar, I was determined to spend one Sunday in town to experience the huge weekly market, when the population of the town swells by many thousands as people stream in on donkey carts, horses, bikes, buses, motorcycles; and in trucks and little red taxis to buy, sell or trade. Kashgar attracts traders from Kazakstan, Kyrgyzstan, Pakistan and even Russia. It is not quite the crossroads trade of Silk Road days, but maintains some of this spirit with people of many nationalities selling everything from carpets to caps, ornate knives to kitchen utensils; as well as spices, gold-plated dowry boxes, brightly painted babies' cradles, saddles, whips and pitchforks. I had seen many bazaars in Central Asia, but nothing had prepared me for the sheer size and variety of this market. It was too huge to take in on one day, so I resolved to give my full attention to the trading of animals that took place in an open arena along the muddy banks of the Tuman River.

I arrived early to film the morning traffic. There had been a terrible, big fight somewhere on the floor of the hotel I was staying in, the night before. It was rumoured to have been between some of the Pakistani traders. As I left the next morning someone was trying to wash away a large pool of blood from the concrete outside a door. It had been a fierce fight, apparently. I took a taxi over to the eastern edge of the town where the 'Kashgar International Trade Market of Central and Western Asia' was already starting to buzz. Not everyone arrived on wheels, some unwilling four-legged participants had to be coaxed down the street, driven out of doorways and outdoor cafes and persuaded to stay together as a group until the saleyard was reached. And here, these same participants were lined up nose to nose on a long rope as patient men with hand shears and combs clipped and patted and struggled with unruly fleeces to make their big-bottomed sheep and noisy goats more attractive than those of the next man. Circles of donkeys were fed armloads of greens, for who would want an irritable, hungry donkey? And men struggled to unload heavy cattle from blue trucks that ground in through the narrow gates throwing dust over all and sundry.

By late morning the traffic moving in and out of the arena had reached a crescendo, the sales were in full swing, and money sometimes changed hands even before the truckloads of animals had made it through the gates. At the edge of this mayhem stood a few old men with three or four forlorn looking sheep. I wanted someone to buy their animals. Men picked up sheep to test them for weight, checked their mouths and clasped hands as money was exchanged. Goats were thrown bodily onto the back of a truck — the billygoat panicking as his women were taken away. Donkeys were led on the trot in a circle to show off their elegant gait, and cattle protested loudly at the indignity of it all. Soon the dust was as thick as porridge, hanging in choking clouds. Mindful of the delicate camera equipment I was carrying, I retreated to the other side of the river to observe from a distance. Standing on the far side of the rickety wooden bridge over the river, I watched as a man chased a runaway horse. It leapt into the river and paddled downstream, and made the mistake of clambering up onto the bank too soon and being caught, only to escape again and be captured once more. It was a very determined horse, angry at having lost its chance of escape.

I met up with Talat in the carpet market, and we escaped to the peace and quiet of the Uyghur burial ground on the outskirts of town. It was enormous, a soft pattern of mostly unmarked graves of adobe, the sun-dried clay shaped into simple dome-covered structures. One structure merged gracefully into the next, and some areas were separated by low mud brick walls. Talat said Uyghur people had been buried here up to 800 years ago, and that the locations of family graves are passed on by oral tradition. Some graves had large, shaped openings, allowing the dry desert air to keep the adobe structure of the tombs intact. Talat described religious occasions when thousands of Uyghur people came here to pray, dance, shout and cry; to have their spirits strengthened and to offer prayers of intercession for loved ones. A few trees dotted the mellow, sculptural landscape. They were planted next to the tombs to remember the name of God so that 'The Name' could be uttered when family and friends could not be there. This was an animistic concept that seemed perfect in this setting, where the manmade tombs, their earthen colours glowing softly in the late afternoon sunshine, appeared seamlessly connected to the earth from which they were created.

Over the Rim of Central Asia

It was now early September — time to set off on the last leg of my journey. At the Chini Bagh Hotel early one morning I lined up for the local Pakistani bus that would make the two-day trip over the Khunjerab Pass, via the Karakoram Highway, a road that has been blasted through some of the world's most formidable mountain ranges where two tectonic plates, the Indian and the Asian, are still grinding together to push the surrounding mountains up even higher. It is a physically volatile area. There are frequent earthquakes along this fault line, heavy snows from May to November, and floods and landslides that periodically close the road. The recent floods that had so devastated the valleys below the Torugart Pass had also wreaked havoc on the Karakoram Highway, ripping out bridges, tumbling huge boulders across the road and collapsing areas of roadway as the grey Ghez River roared through the gorges. The road took twenty years to construct, in a civil engineering project that has been likened to the building of the pyramids. The armies of both Pakistan and China carried out the construction work and fought a war, not without casualties, against the landscape. It has been estimated about four hundred people died building the 1200 kilometres of two-lane roadway. It is an awe-inspiring, fearsomely beautiful 1200 kilometres.

It was a mixed crowd waiting for the bus — half a dozen Pakistani traders, two elderly Uyghur couples on their way to Mecca, their first visit to the holy land and a supremely important journey for them I was told, and a small group of foreign travellers — backpackers. I hadn't met many other backpackers on this journey. Most of my destinations were off even the backpacker trail except for Uzbekistan, so it was usually with great enthusiasm I greeted fellow travellers who spoke English, longing for conversation that wasn't stilted in the search for the right words or the right pronunciation. But it puzzled me that Western tourists who were ready with wide smiles for local people, willingly nursing small children on crowded buses, making attempts at conversation with the adults, found it so difficult to do the same for fellow travellers. There seemed to be an element of competitiveness particularly among backpackers about who could have the best local experience — who could order lunch with ease, who had taken the most difficult route? Perhaps I too had indulged in these vanities. It was something to be aware of.

As the small bus pulled up at the hotel, the line became a huddle around the unopened back door, as the door slowly creaked open the huddle became a rugby scrum and I was pushed rudely to the side by the two biggest Pakistanis who grabbed the best seats at the front where legs could be stretched out in comfort. Other people tried to climb over the top of me. As we would be crossing from China into Pakistan on this journey, the bus would make an overnight stop at Tashkurgan for border formalities. I was glad I had decided to break the trip with another overnight stay. I would go as far as Karakul on the first day, sleep in a guest yurt at the lakeside, and pick up another local bus the following morning. Karakul is Uyghur for 'Black Lake'. Tucked in between two giants of the Pamir Range, the knot of mountains which converge with the Karakoram and the western Himalayas to form the 'Roof of the World', its foreshores are sparsely populated by Kyrgyz herders. Behind the lake soars Mount Kongor with no fewer than eleven glaciers descending its slopes, and on the other side the pyramid-shaped Mount Muztagh Ata rises to 7719 metres. Muztagh Ata is the mountain the Kyrgyz believe to be the site of Shambhala.

It was an easy two-hour ride across the desert towards the snow-covered peaks glinting in the distance, until we entered the canyon of the Ghez River. Here, the ravages of the recent floods made the traversing of huge boulder fields and around walls of deep red sandstone as interesting as it was beautiful. The occasional mud-brick hut sat insignificantly on the immense landscape. Past a checkpoint at Ghez, we entered a vast, solitary, austere land of jagged granite peaks and sheer rock walls, and scree fanning across steep mountainsides. We edged around huge rock falls and along narrow tracks of road that seemed to have been etched out of the solid rock. The river was far below. It was as though the mountains were pressing into the sides of our bus, but I felt suspended in time — light, as if I could will a safe passage for the vehicle and its heavy cargo across the treacherous terrain. No wonder they could only bring the small buses through here. Suddenly the canyon opened out onto a huge plateau dotted with pools of water. We passed a truck lying on its back like a huge cast animal, its wheels still slowly turning. A group of men were climbing in and out of the cab like ants. It was unclear whether anyone had been hurt. A reflection of snow-covered mountains hung in the still water of large pools by the roadside, and ringing the back of the plateau were huge sand dunes, a strange, remarkable sight at nearly 4000 metres above sea level.

It was late afternoon and bitterly cold by the time we reached Karakul. The mountain tops were covered with swirling grey clouds, the glaciers appearing beneath them looked grey too and the waters of the lake were like slate. There were no birds, just a few horses and *dzhos* (a cross between a cow and a yak), and a bored-looking camel outside the restaurant where two large groups of French tourists were dining. The food was too expensive for me to eat both dinner and breakfast there. It seemed likely the restaurant owners had taken good advantage of the half-day's travel between this and the next settlement, but their prices were beyond my very meagre means. I went for a walk in the freezing wind, then unpacked my sleeping bag inside the yurt and tried to sleep. As night wore on I got up to put on more and more clothes, finally pulling my hat down over my face and curling into a foetal ball to escape the gusts of cold wind that blasted through the gaps in the yurt. This certainly didn't feel like Shambhala. Forced outside at midnight by a full bladder, the lake looked grim, the mountains towering behind it like stern sentinels forbidding entry to the land of the gods.

But the morning dawned clear, bright and windless; and as the sun climbed over the mountains its warmth drew me out of the yurt to see a landscape that made me smile with pure pleasure. Fresh snow mantled the mountains, the glaciers glinting in the morning light. The lake was still, unruffled, a deep, deep blue and behind it soared the magnificent shape of Muztagh Ata, with not even a wisp of cloud to mask its outline. I ate breakfast quickly, packed my gear and went for a long walk. Kyrgyz men from the village were already at work, scything the grasses around the foreshore of the lake, their tall white felt hats a familiar silhouette against the backdrop of the mountain's lower flanks. At the lakeside I met two Kyrgyz boys, their faces tanned like leather from the harsh dry air, wind and sun. They sang songs for me, demanding that I sing to them in return so I quickly re-adapted 'Summertime'.

Summertime, but the living's not easy,
Weather's turning, and the snow is well nigh,
Your daddy's not rich,
but your mama's good-looking,
So hush, little baby, don't you cry.

It didn't seem to matter that we couldn't understand each other. A New Zealand Maori love song seemed appropriate too, it involved a lake and it was a pretty song, but when they wanted me to dance as well I thought I'd leave them in their sunny hollow by the shore and see about catching the next bus to Pakistan. With the misery of the previous night's cold forgotten, I turned to look back at the gleaming mountain. Now it was easy to imagine why this place would have been given spiritual significance. It was extraordinarily beautiful, and utterly peaceful. But the mountain hadn't been so kind to a group of climbers who had just returned, disconsolate, to the group of yurts. The gods had denied them the summit, and given one of them a nasty case of frostbite.

Breakfast the following day was a solitary celebration of my fifty-second birthday. I bought warm bread from a tiny bakery in the main street of Tashkurgan, our last stop before Pakistan, and sneaked into the hotel where the bus was parked to find boiling water for a cup of instant coffee — a birthday treat that someone had thoughtfully provided back in Kashgar. I had been given two sachets of coffee, and carefully tucked the second one into my moneybelt with my passport, as a treasure to be saved for later in the day. Tashkurgan is the administrative centre of the Tajik Autonomous County where Tajikistan, Afghanistan and China meet. It is a Tajik town with one main street with loudspeakers dangling from poles crackling irritating broadcasts in Chinese, and more than the usual number of cafes and rundown hotels.

We had arrived in Tashkurgan at dusk. The air was full of smoke from the cafe fires on the footpath. Fellow travellers, a Slovenian couple who had cycled the Karakoram Highway in the opposite direction, directed me to the Ice Mountain Hotel where I was given a very squeaky, saggy little bed in a large double room. I hoped no one would have to sleep in the room with me so that I need not inhibit the tossing and turning I indulged in when overtired and stiff from a long bus journey like this one, which was dragged out by frequent prayer stops for Pakistani traders, toilet stops and punctured tyres. Also at the top of the plateau west of Muztagh Ata, with Tajikistan about ten kilometres away, we stopped again to unload a large piece of machinery that had been lodged in the doorway since I got on at Karakul. I ate in the only cafe that had an English menu, and then fell into bed. I slept restlessly, but was happy that at least there was a trickle of hot water for a birthday shower in the morning.

Chinese immigration procedures were carried out in a huge centre just south of Tashkurgan. I had imagined delays, faultfinding with paperwork and a full luggage inspection, but it was all straightforward — for the foreigners. It took two hours for the Uyghurs on the bus to be cleared. The same officials who had smiled and waved the backpackers through were surly, demanding and officious with these people. Possibly their paperwork was not in order, but I had a sneaking suspicion, unfounded of course, that I was simply witnessing a deeply ingrained racist attitude by the ruling majority towards a minority people. It was not attractive to watch. We waited outside in the sunshine while the luggage was loaded again onto the roof of the bus, although one of the Pakistanis, who had bought himself a new Chinese bicycle, wouldn't allow anyone else to tie it up. He had spent the two waiting hours lovingly cleaning it, stroking it proudly and even allowing a Chinese border policeman to ring the bell. He resembled my image of a Hobbit, a short man in a *shalwar kameez* (knee-length shirt and baggy trousers) with a long black beard and piercing black eyes. When everything else had been securely tied, he hoisted the bicycle onto his shoulder, carefully mounted the ladder to the roof and laying the bicycle down gently, tramped around on top of everyone's luggage to find the best spot for his bike. When it too had been tied down he carefully inspected it for scratches, rang the bell a few times and was finally coaxed back down the ladder. The Uyghurs were through; we were ready to leave for Pakistan.

I was going home at last, but paradoxically I felt I was leaving my home behind me as we climbed up onto the rim of Central Asia, towards the Khunjerab Pass. It was as if I were living the final verses of an epic poem. Dag Hammarskjold's words in *Markings* summed it up:

> … for all the time the journey has already taken,

> how you have needed every second of it in order
> to learn what the road passes by.[13]

On this journey, I often experienced a strong sense of familiarity — in meetings with people, in the places I visited, even in the insights I gained. I came to realise that the teachings of Shambhala are part of our deepest nature and not something we can go out and get. We have a feeling of recognition of our natural state, hidden under our egocentric behaviour and the anxieties and pressures of our everyday existence. When we step out on the path of discovery we are presented with opportunities to rediscover this natural state. We meet people who lead us towards those opportunities and we go to places that stir a deep memory of that state. But of course it's not all easy — where there's renewal there's risk, for a journey without challenge has little meaning.

I was hoping my challenges were almost over, and that I could find a comfortable guesthouse as a base for the next few days — and that night, I hoped to eat a huge Pakistani curry for my birthday dinner. I was tired of the mechanics of travel, the long bus journeys, cramped limbs and lack of good food. Our bus had passed through the level, fertile country alongside the Tashkurgan River, where big herds of *dhzo* grazed placidly — dark, shaggy slow-moving blobs on the landscape — and into a wide, dry valley with just the occasional mud shelter and low stone wall indicating human activity in this high, desolate country. At the top of the valley we had a toilet break and an extended prayer stop. The Pakistani men first set out a melon picnic and then prayed while everyone else waited in the bus. We passed another border post, stopping to deliver two paintbrushes to the border guard and waited again as one of the Pakistanis who had got off for another toilet stop was chased by dogs because he had dared to poke his head into one of the huts. The guards shouted at him and he waved his fist back, a gesture of defiance that seemed to have little meaning and simply held us up again while they demanded to see his papers. I got the impression that these Pakistanis enjoyed living dangerously.

Gradually, grinding our way up through alpine wilderness, we left the Pamir mountains behind and moved into the Karakoram range, on a road that is said to be the highest public highway in the world with the Khunjerab Pass itself at 4730 metres. On the flat land at the top of the pass was a lonely Pakistan security post, where cheerful guards let me film, and everyone trooped out of the bus for a look. We were now officially in Pakistan. This region is home to some of the rarest animals in Asia — the big-horned Marco Polo sheep, the snow leopard, brown bears and ibexes. Occasionally I caught a glimpse of a marmot diving for cover as we passed. Nature reserves have been set aside by

Pakistan and China, on both sides of the pass. Hunting is banned and grazing has been restricted since 1975. Down in the valley the landscape became more and more dramatic with black crumbling rock walls; the river tearing through deep residues of gravel, rock and mud; and hairpin bends on the road affording stunning views from the bus as it twisted and turned down into the final gorge.

Here, at sunset, the inevitable breakdown occurred — this time a leaking tyre that couldn't be changed because we had no spare. We had already used it. The bus limped into the security post where we were required to record our names in a ledger. Though they had no spare wheel for us, what they did have, hanging in the trees at the back of the hut, was a snow leopard. Proudly, a man said he had killed it. It was sad and somewhat offensive to think that this beautiful, elusive and rare animal was still being hunted, inside a national park, and obviously with the full knowledge of the security guards. I knew the World Wildlife Fund put money into this park to protect the endangered species, I had seen their logo several times beside the road on the way down, but I had also heard the enforcement of the hunting ban was seriously underfunded. I found it difficult to comprehend such blatant flouting of the law, let alone boasting to foreign tourists of the kill. Despite the leaking tyre, we kept going — towards Sust.

The high hopes I'd had for a birthday curry were

fading as fast as the daylight. At Sust, with our passports stamped and our luggage given a cursory inspection, I joined the other foreigners from the bus for the final 'taxi' ride down to Karimabad in the Hunza district. A slip of a moon appeared illuminating the razor-sharp mountaintops in a dramatic, breathtaking silhouette as we hurtled through the narrow valley in the back of a small, covered Suzuki truck, dust billowing around us. The side benches in the back of the truck were narrow and uncomfortable, the canvas covering the sides of the truck stopped short of the edge of the seat, and occasionally a stinging spray of gravel rattled across that part of my bottom exposed to the elements. It was cold.

Dinner at the guesthouse had just finished when we arrived, but they took pity on us and quickly rustled up curry with vegetables, rice and chapatis — heavenly food after weeks of rice that always tasted of mutton fat. And later, as I was sitting slumped with exhaustion and a full stomach, an apricot pudding appeared, with a candle stuck in the middle. Some kind person had whispered a word in the manager's ear. It was a birthday celebration after all. I felt like crying. I had already chosen my bed, a wooden platform under the stars on the flat roof of the guesthouse. Lying out in my sleeping bag, too tired to sleep; I gazed at the brilliant, unfamiliar northern sky, wondering what my fifty-third year would bring.

Waking at dawn, I sat bolt upright, speechless. The day was cloudless and the first rays of the sun touched the snow-covered peak of Rakoposhi, a giant of the Karakoram that seemed to be looming splendidly right in front of my face. In reality it was across the valley, but the Hunza I'd had lodged in my imagination — a wide, flat valley between distant mountains — was not the Hunza I saw in front of me. This place had immense mountains rising almost vertically from the river, scattered villages perched in impossible places on green terraces dotted with groves of almond, walnut and apricot trees; narrow roadways were lined with poplars that were just showing signs of their autumn colours; and lines of irrigation channels wound around steep slopes, fed from the snows above. Behind me rose the amphitheatre of peaks above Baltit and south-east, the huge mountains of Nagar. I lay on my open wooden platform, engulfed by a great sense of peace, until the sun reached me two hours later.

I spent a few days wandering around the small villages, marvelling at how mountain slopes with few horizontal surfaces had been transformed into fertile gardens — such agriculture made possible with water carried down from high canyons by the intricate system of irrigation channels. Some fields were as much as eight kilometres from the water source. There are no forests in these mountains, but the fast-growing poplar trees provide firewood, timber and even fodder for the animals; and maize and wheat supply the dietary staples. It's a place where heaven and earth meet visually, in the immense sweep from wide river to terraced fields, to exposed mountain walls, to glistening snow-covered peaks; and it's easily accessible for tourists now with the Karakoram Highway — a paved road up the Indus, Gilgit and Hunza river valleys.

I met a lot of other tourists in Hunza, both independent backpackers and those in tour groups, and as I had spent so much time on my own it was challenging being among tourist activity again. My last experience of this had been in Uzbekistan and before that, only in the large and fairly anonymous Chinese cities. It was bewildering how so many people seemed to hold themselves as separate and different; and how detached they seemed to be from their surroundings. Remembering the glassy expressions of tourist groups in Uzbekistan, it occurred to me it might have something to do with the mode of travel. Busloads of people who have everything arranged for them travel with a high degree of certainty, but it is *uncertainty* that sparks the fire of discovery. When things are certain, whether it's in a relationship, or a religion, or on a journey, inertia can creep in and we are not propelled to seek for answers. The only thing that is certain is change itself, and in surrendering to change we are able to have a journey of self-discovery.

~

I had met a young man called Dowar in the Karimabad bazaar, who owned a small shop selling dried fruits and nuts. He was also a poet and musician and invited me to film a musical evening he and his friends were arranging for a group of tourists at one of the local inns. It was a good night — warm, with a quarter-moon shining brightly over the mountains — and the young musicians playing with enthusiasm. Two older men danced proudly, sometimes fiercely, as in the intricate sword dance when their blades seemed to whirl perilously close to vulnerable areas of each other's anatomy. The tourists sat stony-faced on chairs around the perimeter of the grass. Their rare applause seeming grudging and at the end of the show, when everyone was invited to dance, they got up and left without a word of thanks. It was very odd — but perhaps it was simply inertia which kept them so uninvolved. I could consider myself very lucky I'd been unable to take anything for granted on this journey. I danced with Dowar's friend Ali who asked me to marry him at the end of the evening, one of several proposals of marriage I received in Pakistan. My polite refusals were always accepted gracefully when these young men learned how old I was.

I learned to enjoy myself in these surroundings. I was tired enough to appreciate the tourist facilities, the tours to places off the main road in open-topped jeeps, and the English so readily spoken. One day I shared a jeep with two other Westerners for a trip into the former princely state of Nagar on the opposite side of the river, still a beautiful area, but lacking the luminous incandescence of the Hunza landscape. Here, massive peaks loom over the valley throwing bulky shadows of their mighty shapes. The heavier snow of the region provides more water so there is no need for the sophisticated irrigation system of Hunza, but I missed the hand-drawn lines of the stone channels across the face of the mountains. It was as though a painting hadn't quite been finished. Historically, the Hunza and Nagar kingdoms were separate, although from the fifteenth century they were ruled by blood-related families who constantly feuded, even as they intermarried, over the centuries. Both kingdoms were brought into Pakistan after the Partition of 1947 and although the Mir of Nagar still resides in the former capital, Nagar village, his status is now not more than that of district official.

~

At the bottom of a large glacier in the Hoper Valley, high in the Nagar region, I met a group of men who make their living from the precious and semiprecious stones found in these mountains. Some of them had walked for weeks into the mountains to find the stones, taking enough food on their backs and sleeping in caves, tents or huts. Sometimes they blast the rock and sometimes they 'just find' the stones but a young entrepreneur at the glacier told me it was only the older men who did this — those with the knowledge and the stamina! There is no stone-cutting equipment in this region, so over the winter months the rocks are taken down to Peshawar on the Afghan border to be cut and shaped. Selling the stones was purely a summer business. No one came here in winter, and often the men of a village would move down to Rawalpindi or one of the big towns to find work during the cold months.

I found that it was difficult to simply look at items for sale in these tourist-orientated areas, because the unspoken attitude seemed to be if you *look*, you buy. And as much as I would have liked to add rubies, lapis lazuli, tourmaline and garnets to my rock collection at home, I had simply run out of money for non-essential items. But I was also starting to get a niggling feeling that for all the friendliness shown to me by these men and others I had met, I was no longer making the connections with people that had made the rest of the journey so memorable when relationships were based on the genuine interest of one person for another, and not solely on commercial transactions of goods and services.

Perhaps I was just too weary to keep up my part of the exchange. Fed up with the hard sell, I headed back to Hunza. I took to walking in the evenings when shopkeepers had stopped hassling for sales and were sitting drinking tea in groups around the bazaar. Then they were willing to have a chat about their valley and, sometimes, the world beyond their valley. That's how it seemed here — that there was Hunza, and then there was the rest of the world.

But now I knew I was ready to return to my familiar world. I wanted to see my daughter, sleep in my own bed, choose the food I ate and look at the sea again.

~

Gilgit is the largest town in the Northern Areas of Pakistan, and was to be my last stop before Mumbai (formerly Bombay) and my plane back to Sydney. I was at the point where I could imagine myself on that plane, my huge backpack stowed, my mind busy with homecoming scenarios. There were two ways I could travel from Gilgit to Mumbai. The first involved a long and tortuous bus ride down mountain roads, a journey of some fourteen to seventeen hours to Islamabad, and then a plane via Karachi to Mumbai. The second option was to go to Gilgit, book a ticket on the spectacular flight to Islamabad, a one and a quarter hour trip on a Fokker Friendship aeroplane, and pray for clear weather. I hadn't been on a Fokker Friendship since my childhood. Given aeroplanes are passed down to poorer nations as they near the end of their economic life, this could well be the same one. On the route from Gilgit the plane flies to Islamabad between the mountains, close to Nanga Parbat, the eighth-highest mountain in the world. Not surprisingly, near-perfect weather conditions are required. Frequent flight cancellations mean that there is often a backlog of passengers waiting to leave Gilgit. Consequently, every booking has a standby status, and the final decision to fly is only ever made shortly before the scheduled departure time. There was nothing certain about this route, but I had to be in Gilgit to take my chance.

Gilgit, unaffected by tourism, was a pleasant town to wait in. In the first to the third centuries CE it was part of the Kushan Empire which adopted Buddhism. West of the town there is still a large Buddha carved into a cliff face, the ruins of a monastery and stupa, and a cave where Buddhist texts were found in the 1930s. I stayed at the Medina guesthouse, hidden in a garden away from the noise of the town. It was close enough to walk to the airline office and to the local polo ground where Gilgit teams were practising hard for the Uprising Day tournament in November. I watched the play one evening — the muezzin's call to prayer from the nearby mosque mingling with the clash of sticks and shouts from team members. Polo is a simple game. There are only six people on a team, but there are few rules and it's played passionately — fast and furiously. Horses foamed at the mouth, players hung off their saddles to get the best shot, and spectators leapt back as balls and sticks came uncomfortably close to the sideline. A small band of drummers and pipers was on hand to announce each goal scored, and at half-time small boys proudly led the sweating horses around the field to keep them warmed up for the second half. It seemed to be every young boy's dream to be a polo player. In a dusty field next to the mosque a group of boys, long shirts flapping, used improvised sticks, sometimes mimicking the gallop of a horse as they played a high-spirited game of their own.

~

At the airline office I was told that if I came back before 10.00 am on Sunday, I would have a good chance for Monday's flight. Later, I understood I had jumped a queue without realising it. On Sunday morning I walked in to find a scrum of men in the office, waving papers, shouting at the two men behind the desk who looked supremely unmoved at the mayhem in front of them. I decided to sit down and wait for the melee to subside; there was no way I was going to make myself understood across that hubbub. Suddenly I heard my name called among the Husseins et al. and I was handed a ticket for the first flight out in the morning. 'Be at the airport at 6.30 am,' he said sternly. Jaw dropping, I made my thanks and retreated. I couldn't believe my luck.

The day dawned perfectly clear. I went up onto the rooftop of the guesthouse to make absolutely sure of this and yes, there was not a cloud in the sky. In the airport waiting room, having survived the indignity of a thorough body search by a stout dragon of a woman who was possibly checking for weapons, and with my luggage tagged and stamped, I looked out to see our Friendship taxiing quietly up the small runway. The weather had held, we would be leaving.

I felt I could reach out of the windows and touch the mountains. Nanga Parbat floated into view — majestic, a sublime mountain among so many giants; and in the cockpit where I had been allowed to stand and gaze for five minutes, I saw the plains and cities of the lowlands coming to meet us. Central Asia was now far behind me, a still-vivid memory of people and places I was determined to keep intact for as long as I could.

~

Islamabad and Rawalpindi are like twin cities, 15 kilometres apart by road, but planets apart in character and orientation. Islamabad is spread out with open green spaces, wide boulevards and gridded, anonymously numbered streets. Rawalpindi is crammed with bazaars and bustling intersections, narrow streets and a snarl of traffic. My bird's-eye view from the plane, however, showed clearly how these two cities were linked — by a blanket of heat haze and pollution that spread across the two cities like an oppressive weight.

In Rawalpindi the electricity had died — the ceiling fans in the gloomy dormitory bedroom of my hotel, where two Japanese men lay prostrate on their narrow beds, had slowly rotated to a halt, and in the restaurant downstairs it was too dark to see what I was eating for breakfast. I felt suddenly depressed, overdressed and overheated in the modest, long-sleeved dress and baggy trousers required in this overtly Muslim city. There seemed to be no difference between the temperature and humidity outside and that of the hotel room, so I ventured forth into the shrill cacophany of the streets to find my bearings and perhaps a quieter, well-lit cafe in which to sit and write, and organise my thoughts. There were two tasks I could not avoid — organising a visa for India, and a ticket to get there.

I walked down Murree Road towards a hotel I'd been told about. It was out of my price range, but hopefully it would have a bar or cafe where I could pretend to adopt a lifestyle I was now aspiring to: comfort. A jeep was parked at the entrance to the hotel. There were three men in the jeep, and one of them hailed me: 'Hello! Where are you going?' 'Why do you want to know?' I replied. 'Going to Gilgit?' 'No, I've just come from there.' I walked into the hotel to find a cooler place to sit, but the man at the desk obviously knew who his guests were, and wasn't going to let any Western riff-raff through the doors. As I walked back into the heat of the street a tall young man fell into step beside me, the same man who had spoken to me from the jeep. Dressed in a dusty, drab green *shalwar kameez*, he was good-looking with the slightly stooped posture tall people often have. His gaze was intense but pleasant and he spoke English very well. I told him about my desire for a more comfortable hotel, said I had to find a travel agent to book my ticket to Mumbai and he in turn offered to take me to the Sadder bazaar where I would find cheap places for both a room and a ticket.

We drove over in the jeep. Rakesh was confident and even rather languid at the wheel, and seemingly oblivious to the confusion of traffic on all sides. He was a mountain guide, born in one of the mountain villages north of Gilgit that I'd wanted to visit, had I the time. Now, like many men of the Northern Areas, he made his living guiding tourists around the popular destinations off the Karakoram Highway — the base camps of the high mountains, the glaciers and high passes. He smoked furiously and intently.

I wondered how he kept up the level of fitness necessary for the high altitudes, but kept my mouth shut. It was none of my business.

His favourite travel agent was closed, but the hotel where he stayed, within my price range and with a good restaurant, had rooms to spare. It had a 'bar' serving tea and instant coffee with a balcony overlooking the street, a marvellous spot for observing (without being observed) the endless stream of humanity which passed through the busy bazaar. It was wonderful to feel anonymous, but evidently 'anonymous' was not what Rakesh had in mind. The talk soon turned to men–women relationships, Pakistan-style, and thence to sex, and quickly to the suggestion I might spend some time with him and have some fun. I didn't need too long to think about his proposal — he was, he said, thirty years old; he was very attractive and obviously had no qualms about side-stepping the guidelines of the predominant faith of his country. Nor did he blink an eye when I told him how old I was. I decided I could do with some fun myself after almost five months of intense work and physical hardship.

At the main desk I filled out my foreigner's registration form, quietly observing the exchange of sly little smiles between the desk clerks. Perhaps this was a common routine, but I didn't care what Rakesh got up to at other times, as long as he looked after me. My small, plain room had doors opening onto a balcony, but it didn't help to relieve the suffocating heat of the evenings because Rakesh insisted on closing and locking all doors, and plugging the keyholes to prevent anyone from spying on us. It was probably a reasonable apprehension, but the precautions extended from the bedroom to every facet of life in the hotel until the affair took on the quality of a charade — a most amusing and enjoyable deception as far as I was concerned. It was difficult to know what Rakesh was thinking or feeling. He was a very intense and serious man, but occasionally, with a sudden clap of his hands, he would break into a shout of laughter when something struck him as being particularly funny. It was important to be seen to meet 'accidentally' in the restaurant for breakfast each morning, and to appear surprised and delighted to see each other, and outside the privacy of the bedroom I had to remember to keep my hands to myself, sitting with at least one spare seat between us. Rakesh said he couldn't dance, yet at the first notes of a favourite musician he'd leap up, swaying his angular body between the dining tables, head thrown back and fingers snapping, sometimes softly crooning the notes of the song. I liked him enormously. He appeared to live life on his own terms within the confines of the rigid societal framework, yet he was a scrupulously honourable man in his dealings with others, and obviously respected despite his penchant for foreign women. I was under no illusion that I was the only one.

And so I found myself being looked after and cared for in a most unexpected and delightful way. The transient nature of the relationship was immaterial and, if anything, added a certain piquancy to those few days, but the knowledge that someone was 'there for me' created a safe retreat at a time when I was feeling particularly vulnerable. It had been difficult obtaining an Indian visa at short notice. I had almost been arrested as a spy for filming in the street opposite the Ministry of Defence building, although it wasn't obviously identified as such, and I was preoccupied, filming one of the gloriously decorated, densely packed Pakistani buses. A very angry man had stormed up, almost knocking the camera over. 'Are you a spy?' he shouted. 'Don't be ridiculous,' I said, 'What is this building?' 'I'm not going to tell you what this building is, you are a *spy*!' I packed my camera and tripod up with as much dignity as I could muster and stalked off back to the hotel, thankful he had not broken my camera or even confiscated the tape I was finishing as it was full of beautiful Hunza images. The name of the building was written in large letters on the gate further down the street, but I had never given it a thought. This was a town to be careful in.

~

The cheap flight to Mumbai left at midnight and had a stopover in Karachi of several hours. Rakesh didn't mention my imminent departure, but over dinner that evening his long, unwavering gazes and mercurial behaviour intensified, and I felt genuine regret at our parting. I couldn't even give him a hug to say goodbye. He rode a little way in the taxi with me, leapt out at his favourite cafe, kissed the air, and was gone. At 2.00 am I was in Karachi at the huge new, gleaming airport terminal, with the top zip on my pack undone and my camera cleaning kit gone. I was refused entry by rifle-carrying guards at the international departure lounge because I was too early, so I sat in the restaurant where people lay asleep on beds fashioned from several chairs, and talked to a young Pakistani businessman. He was going to marry soon, he said, and planned to go to Canada to live because Pakistan and its president were now ruled by the military and the country was suffering badly. I'd heard that over forty per cent of the population lived under the poverty line, but he said it was more like ninety per cent.

At 4.00 am the restaurant closed and I made my way back to the international lounge which had just opened for business. I was grumpy with fatigue. The customs officials had set up a table near the main doors and proceeded to take every single item out of my pack, deliberately and slowly and, I felt, in a rather insulting manner. A packet of tampons had broken open, and just as I was beginning to feel very irritated by the lengthy, drawn-out proceedings, a tampon was held up by the string, cotton wad dangling. 'What is this?' the official said sternly. How could I explain without getting arrested? Fighting back hysterical laughter I tried to indicate the personal nature of the items, whereupon the whole packet was unceremoniously dumped on top of everything else, in full view of anyone who entered the building. I didn't want an unpleasant Karachi airport experience to sour my view of Pakistan so I bit my tongue, gathered my things together and repacked, slowly and methodically, at the customs table, watched by the gun-toting guards.

From Karachi I flew to Mumbai. I arrived, coincidentally, for the final day of the ten-day festival of Ganesh, the elephant-headed god of wisdom and success, and the defender and remover of obstacles. The god is also no stranger to epics. In Indian mythology Ganesh is said to have written down the *Mahabharata* in one sitting, so I felt it was auspicious to have arrived for the culmination of the festival, when hundreds of statues of this god are immersed in the sea at Chowpatty Beach. The final lines of *my* epic were being written noisily on all sides of me. It was a riotous occasion. Bands and a sea of dancers and revellers accompanied the statues through the streets to the beach, some after long journeys into the city. For hours that same evening whistle blowing and shouting heralded the progress of the statues down to the water's edge, where the tide was slowly covering the sand. Some of the statues were enormous, others were modest family offerings. All were given up to the dissolving action of the water with joy and reverence, a symbolic acknowledgement of the rhythm of change in our lives. Opportunity comes, and it goes; wisdom is gained or not gained. We can either take it, or leave it.

The celebration of Ganesh felt like a completion to my journey, a symbolic recognition of the nature of journeys. My search for Shambhala had taken a long and circuitous route around the major mountain ranges of Central Asia, and although I didn't find the legendary earthly paradise, along the way many special people had offered the very qualities I associated with Shambhala, those of kindness, compassion and fraternity. And perhaps more importantly, the journey had offered the opportunities to find those same qualities in myself, a chance to develop 'Shambhala warriorship' as Chogyam Trungpa calls it, letting go of fixed mindsets and trying to respond in a spontaneous, light way to whatever was offered.

And what could I give back? Teachers from all of the world's great religions and philosophies have spoken of the gift of increased self-knowledge, of hard-earned wisdom, but it's not easy to bestow that gift without appearing arrogant and self-involved. I had a film to make, a story to be told in images and with a brief narrative, but my feeling was that the real jewels were the hidden stories — the tales from the heart of the journey, recorded privately in my journals and still intensely fresh in my mind. I decided to write a book about my journey, offering it as an expression of gratitude for the things I was taught.

Epilogue

When I returned to Sydney I soon realised I would have to deal with the grief I felt over my mother's death, most of which had been pushed away to enable me to keep focused on the filming. As soon as I stopped moving my grief erupted into a constricted, painful throat infection that even antibiotics couldn't shift. Finally I tried a non-medical approach and went to see a woman who I was told could heal psychically, through the intervention of non-mortal beings. After the session, she described in detail one of the men who had 'spoken' to her, saying he wished to be made known to me. I thought I recognised the yogi whose photograph was on the front cover of his autobiography, a book I'd picked up from a secondhand stall, and had carried around for at least ten years, without ever opening it. Finding the book still tucked away I dusted it off and read it. It was a revelation. Yogananda Paramahansa had pointed me firmly towards the journey I was now ready for — the spiritual path of yoga and the teachings of Shambhala.

I travelled to New Zealand to scatter my mother's ashes with my siblings, waiting until low tide on the beach at the front of the house, making sure the rock pools and small waves received a good spread of her bodily remains. Saying goodbye to the house at Ruby Bay was one of the most difficult things I have ever done, and I thought my heart would break. Back in Sydney I was offered an art-teaching position, and I started training to be a yoga teacher. I was introduced to a group of like-minded people, and began singing sacred yogic texts with them and felt my throat respond to the expansive sounds of the chants. Yoga philosophy classes started opening me up to new ways of engaging with other people and the events of my life. Art and yoga — the springboards for a journey that will engage me for the rest of this life.

I know other places will call me away again and offer their unique experiences, and I'm certain that whatever I gain from them will be cloaked in the teachings of Shambhala. Sometimes I feel I am a most fortunate woman, but this is not just my path — it belongs to everyone. We are all on the sacred mountain, and all we have to do is keep ascending.

Notes

1 Frederic Prokosch, *Seven Who Fled,* Farrar, Straus & Giroux, New York, 1984. p. 5.

2 Chogyam Trungpa, *Shambhala: The Sacred Path of the Warrior*, Shambhala Publications, Boston, 1984. p. 27.

3 Mildred Cable, with Francesca French, *The Gobi Desert*, Beacon Press, Boston, 1942. p. 58.

4 Henning Haslund, *Men and Gods in Mongolia,* Adventures Unlimited Press, Stelle, Ill., 1992. pp. 6–7.

5 Sogyal Rinpoche, *The Tibetan Book of Living and Dying*, ed. Patrick Gaffney and Andrew Harvey, Rider, Random House, Australia, 1992.

6 Victoria Le Page, *Shambhala*, The Theosophical Publishing House, Wheaton, Ill., 1996. p. 156.

7 Chogyam Trungpa. op. cit. p. 174.

8 Untitled short poem by William Blake from *The English Galaxy of Shorter Poems,* ed. by G. Bullett, J. M. Dent and Sons, London, 1933. p. 341.

9 Frederic Prokosch, op. cit.

10 Chogyam Trungpa. op. cit. p. 96.

11 Chogyam Trungpa. op. cit. p. 132.

12 Chogyam Trungpa. ibid. p. 48.

13 Dag Hammarskjold, *Markings*, Random House, New York, 1988. p. 172.

Bibliography

A Traveller's Companion to Central Asia, Kathleen Hopkirk. John Murray, London, 1997.

Central Asia; A Lonely Planet Travel Survival Kit, John King, John Noble and Andrew Humphreys. Lonely Planet Publications, Melbourne, 1996.

China, Robert Story, Nicko Goncharoff, Damien Harper, Marie Cambon, Thomas Huhti, Caroline Liou and Alexander English. Lonely Planet Publications, Melbourne, 1998.

Foreign Devils on the Silk Road, Peter Hopkirk, Oxford University Press, Oxford, New York, 1980.

Men and Gods in Mongolia, Henning Haslund, Adventures Unlimited Press, Stelle, Ill., 1992.

Mongolia, Paul Greenway, Robert Storey and Gabriel Lafitte, Lonely Planet Publications, Melbourne, 1997.

Pakistan, John King, Bradley Mayhew and David St Vincent, Lonely Planet Publications, Melbourne, 1998.

Shambhala, Victoria LePage, Quest Books, Theosophical Publishing House, Wheaton, Ill., 1996.

Shambhala; The Sacred Path of the Warrior, Chogyam Trungpa, Shambhala Publications, Boston, Mass., 1984.

The Art of Pilgrimage: The Seeker's Guide to Making Travel Sacred, Phil Cousineau, Conari Press, Berkeley, California, 1998.

The Elements of Shamanism, Nevill Drury, Element Books, Dorset, 1989.

The Ends of the Earth: A Journey at the Dawn of the 21st Century, Robert D. Kaplan, Random House, New York, 1996.

Index